These essays and illustrations originally ran in six consecutive issues of *Green Book* magazine, from February through July of 1918.

To the best of the publisher's research and knowledge, these essays and illustrations are in the public domain. Anyone with reason to believe otherwise is asked to contact the publisher.

The editing, new coloring of covers, and any other new material in this book is Copyright © 2016 by Rodney Schroeter. All rights reserved. Errors in the source material have been corrected, thus making the text as published here easily distinguishable from the original, and not in the public domain. Except for brief passages for intellectually rigorous articles or reviews, no portion of this book may be reproduced in any form or by any mechanical, electronic or other means, now known or hereafter invented, possible or impossible, rational or irrational, including photocopying, xerography and recording, or in any information retrieval system without the express written permission of the publisher. Book pirates (print or electronic) are advised to cease and desist before they even contemplate commencement, and to walk the planks into their own moral sewers. However, the reader is cheerfully encouraged to commit this text in its entirety to memory, in anticipation for the time when its ownership is adjudged to be illegal, immoral, and/or fattening.

This is text version 1.0. Anyone bringing errors in this text to the publisher's attention will be credited in later versions.

Illustrations by William Oberhardt.

The Woman Tamers
ISBN: 978-0-9967194-5-2 (paperback)
ISBN: 978-1-945307-01-0 (ebook)

Book compilation and design by Rodney Schroeter

The Silver Creek Press
PO Box 334
Random Lake WI 53075-0334
rschroeter@silentreels.com

The Woman Tamers

by
Albert Payson Terhune

Illustrated by William Oberhardt

Silver
Creek
Press

2016

Table of Contents

I. Lord Byron
   The Lame Charlatan Who Enslaved
      Every Woman He Met 7

II. Napoleon
   Conqueror of Thrones and Women 19

III. Jonathan Swift
   The Great Bear
      of Love and Literature 29

IV. Alexandre Dumas
   The Monte Cristo Heart-Breaker 39

V. Marshal Saxe
   The Swashbuckling Heart-Breaker 51

VI. Frédéric Chopin
   Invalid Heartbreaker 63

Appendix
   Source Material Notes 73

I — Lord Byron

The Lame Charlatan
Who Enslaved Every Woman He Met

A YELLOW-FACED boy—club-footed, fat and untidy—became, in 1798, through the death of his rascally great-uncle, a baron. The lad was George Gordon Byron.

He was ten when he came into his high-sounding title and a tumbledown country seat at Newstead, England, along with the tattered remnant of a fortune which his ancestors had industriously been squandering in every possible form of vice. Up to that time he and his half-crazy shrew of a mother had scraped along as best they could on a beggarly pension.

Byron's right foot was shrunken and twisted by infantile paralysis. His childhood was further made miserable by his mother, who alternately fondled him and screamed curses at him. He hated her—though, after her unlamented death, he spoke snivelingly of her as his "one friend." There was insanity on both sides of the family, and violent temper and dissipation as well. So Byron did not start life well equipped.

His first love-affair—recorded by himself—was at the age of seven. He adored one Mary Duff, an Aberdeen girl some years his senior. He never saw her again. But nine years later, when he heard she had married a wholesale wine-merchant named Coburn, he burst into tears. In after-life he once said:

"I never enjoy drinking Coburn's port. It reminds me too much of Mary."

The next affair was when he had reached the advanced age of twelve. The girl was his cousin Margaret Parkes. She died, in early youth, from an accident to her spine. And again Byron cried. He was much given to tears at this period—almost as much as to causing them, later on.

Then, at fifteen, came the real romance of his life. At first glance it seems a mere calf-love episode, but it had results that were far-reaching.

The Chaworth estate adjoined his. And he proceeded to fall in love with Mary Chaworth—a dreamy, selfish, fluff-brained girl two years his senior. Nearly always Byron's sweethearts were older than he. (Byron's worthless great-uncle, by the way, had killed Mary's father in a duel.)

Mary—at that period—just amused herself with Byron, teasing him, flirting heartlessly with him and all the time secretly listening to the love-vows of John Masters, a neighboring squire. One day Byron called on Mary. While he was waiting for her, he overheard another girl and herself chatting in the next room. The other girl was guying Mary about Byron's attentions. Mary laughed aloud, and Byron heard her exclaim:

"Are you goose enough to suppose I could ever fall in love with that funny fat lame brat?"

Byron rushed from the house, weeping in anguish. Soon afterward Mary was married to Masters—who promptly developed into a heavy drinker and who used to beat her with great regularity. Yet the affair was not ended. It twisted the whole current of the sensitive boy's life. Henceforth he wept for no woman, but he made plenty of them weep for him.

"This hapless love of his for Mary Chaworth," writes his friend and biographer Gribble, "was the dominating influence of his life. He never loved any other woman. His later love-affairs were only attempts to escape from himself and from his memories."

It seems ridiculous that a silly romance at fifteen should have shaped a man's after-life. But it was true, with Byron. It not only started the vein of

The Woman Tamers

melancholy that runs through all his work and set him to scribbling poetry, but it made him immune to any other girl's charms. This indifference, as well as his air of mysterious melancholy, at once waked women to keen interest in him.

He was frightfully sensitive about his fat and his lameness. Mary's sneer at them moved him to cure both. He went to a high-priced quack to have his clubfoot treated. The quack tortured him and left him no better off than before. So he turned to athletics to build up his body. In spite of his lameness he soon became a crack swimmer and boxer and cricket-player. Athletics also began to take down his fat. Byron helped along this process by eating potatoes drenched in vinegar and by drinking quarts of Epsom salts.

As a result, by the time he went to Cambridge, he had a good figure and a villainous digestion. At Cambridge his income amounted to twenty-five hundred dollars a year. He not only spent this but ran into debt, to the sum of sixteen thousand dollars besides. He had a decidedly merry time at Cambridge. He used to say he had turned to spendthrift dissipation in order to forget Mary. This excuse is as good as another.

One man in a thousand is a born woman-tamer. And he is a born woman-tamer, for no reason that his less lucky fellow-men can find out.

To make extra money, he also made use of his Mary-blighted affections to turn out reams of verse about his broken heart.

Let me stop here, a moment, to say that Byron was a blackguard, a charlatan and a man of silly poses, but that he was also one of the few immortal poets the literary universe has thus far known. Too many modernists scoff at his verse and call it old-fashioned. But it is the most beautiful and deathless poetry of its sort ever written. And, with all his vices and affectations, he was as hard a worker at his writing-trade as any man on earth. He slaved as steadily as a day-laborer.

And now—though it belongs later in the story—let us finish with Mary Chaworth.

BYRON came back to England after a long absence and at once acquired more glamorous notoriety than any other man alive. Women went mad over him. Men aped his careless attire, his air of gloom and his loose low collars and looser, lower morals. With this atmosphere of romance about him and with his growing fame as a woman tamer, he met Mary again. Their estates adjoining, they were close neighbors. And both of them proceeded to obey the Scriptural injunction, "Love thy neighbor."

Mary, by this time, was thoroughly disillusioned with Masters. Nor, perhaps, was she as lovely as when Byron had sighed in vain for her favor. No longer was she the all-conquering village belle and he the fat young nonentity. She was merely the comely spouse of Squire Masters, and Byron was world-famous and courted. The old state of their relations was reversed. Mary was vastly flattered to be wooed by a man whom all other women worshiped, and she met his advances more than halfway. (At that, she had not far to travel.)

Byron loved her. He said so, in verse and in prose, in letter and by word of mouth—to Mary and to several of their friends. He could not love anybody as much as he loved himself; yet he loved Mary more than he loved any of his other flames. Perhaps this was because she was almost the only girl who had not succumbed to him at once—perhaps, too, there was as much revenge as love in his courtship. It was a cheap revenge, but it was the sort in which Byron's soul delighted: once, Mary had flouted him; now it was a keen satisfaction to bring her to his feet.

Their estates being so close together, there was no difficulty in choosing a woodland trysting-place whither Masters was not likely to stroll. There the lovers met. The meetings continued for weeks. At last some considerate friend hinted to Masters that his wife had distressingly few traits in common with Caesar's. Byron avoided worse scandal by going away. Mary followed him to London and to one or two watering-places—apparently through her own wish, not at his.

And again the affair was taken up where it had been left off. But again Masters' suspicions were aroused—this time by a letter of Mary's that fell into his hands.

Mary, in mortal terror, appealed to Byron to save her. Instead he left her in the lurch. He wrote to several people about this new peril to his precious life. To one he wrote:

> I fear I must hold myself in readiness for a challenge from the husband, unless I withdraw. While I can split a wafer with a pistol-ball, yet this husband is in the right. I have wronged him. Therefore I shall do what I can to avert any condition in which I may have to kill him. There is talk, I hear, of his forcing a duel on me.

Out of belated consideration for Masters' safety—or out of chronic solicitude for his own—Byron left Mary to the mercy of her hard-drinking and justly jealous spouse and took himself out of her life. But he went on writing—and selling—poems about her for years thereafter. Mary subsided into a life of seclusion and of patient misery—from which she is said to have emerged with pathetic eagerness at the beck of Byron's finger, when once he deigned to take up her acquaintance again. But he abandoned her almost at once, and as capriciously as he had restored her into momentary favor.

Still, the fact remains that she is the only one of his loves to whom he ever returned after once dismissing her—and that he risked death at Masters' pistol (until the liaison began to grow wearisome) to carry on the fierce intrigue with this love of his first youth.

All of this carries us far ahead of our story—from which we digressed at the point where Byron was horrifying his sedater comrades at Cambridge.

ONE affair followed hot on the heels of another, after Byron left Cambridge. He wrote love-poems to these new sweethearts, vowing eternal fidelity to each of them—and then collecting the poems in a book and selling them. (He wrote one poem too many, by the way, a poem praising Napoleon—who was just then England's arch-enemy. It was received in London much as a poem applauding the Kaiser would to-day be received in New York.)

Byron, meanwhile, was having a beautiful time. In the intervals between his lurid love-affairs, he used to entertain stag-parties at

Newstead. There, clad in monks' robes, the guests and host would spend the night drinking Burgundy from a human skull. They went to bed at three in the morning and arose at one in the afternoon. Nor were all the parties strictly "stag."

Presently, Byron decided that this kind of life was too monotonous. So he left England, for a loafing-tour of Europe and the East. Always posing, he hinted darkly that a mysterious crime or a perilous love-affair was driving him into exile. There is no proof of either. He was ever an arrant liar.

At Seville, soon after he set forth on his travels, Byron met the daughter of Admiral Cordova. She was the original of *Haidee* in his "Don Juan." He wrote thus of her to his mother:

> She honored your unworthy son with very particular attentions, embracing him with great tenderness, at parting—after cutting off a lock of his hair and presenting him with one of her own, about three feet long.

The letter ends with further details of the flirtation, which are far too glaringly intimate for reproduction here and which, if true, brand the man as a cur for telling of them.

Many women—like the Admiral's daughter—gave Byron locks of their hair. From the number of locks *he* parted with, it is a miracle he was not bald. This mystery may be cleared up, though, by the statement that several of his successive valets had hair of the same general color as his own, and that all women were not shrewd enough to make sure of the lock's authenticity by cutting it off his head in person.

At Malta he met Mrs. Spenser Smith, wife of a British ambassador. Just what happened nobody knows. But in "Childe Harold" Byron mentions her by her first name and informs the world at large that she made love to him which he did not think it worth his while to return.

Thence he went to Greece. There, at the Greek capital, he stopped at lodgings kept by Theodora Macri, the widow of a British vice-consul. Mrs. Macri had a dark-eyed daughter named Teresa. Byron wasted no time in starting a romance with Teresa, and when he was about to move on to Constantinople, he wrote a poem of farewell to her. It began:

> Maid of Athens, ere we part,
> Give, oh, give me back my heart.

Yes, it was the same old "Maid of Athens" lyric that our grandparents used to warble. And it made the chaste Teresa's fortune. For the poem sprang into instant fame, and it brought shoals of tourists to Mrs. Macri's house. The thrifty landlady ran up her prices and always had a long waiting-list.

So much revenue and reputation did "Maid of Athens" bring in, that Greece at last pensioned Teresa. She traded long on her beauty and Byronic fame. At last she married an English diplomat named Black. She lived to be eighty—still shining in the reflected glory of one short love-song.

NEAR Athens, too,—according to a story he himself told,—Byron was one day riding along the seashore when he met a crowd of men carrying a sack. In the sack was a beautiful Turkish girl who for some misdemeanor was about to be cast into the sea. Byron, at the pistol-point, rescued her from her captors and sent her to her relatives at Thebes. But because he would not go to Thebes with her, she pined, and soon died of a broken heart. (Eddie Foy would doubtless say of the story: "'Tis a pretty thing.")

On his way back, at Malta, Byron met a Mrs. Pedley, the gay wife of an army surgeon. She loved Byron devotedly—though, it was said, not exclusively. Mistaking the poet's gallantry and taking his vows at their face value, she left her husband and one morning walked in on Byron bag and baggage, and announced she had come to stay.

Byron, terribly embarrassed, explained to her that she had quite misunderstood him, and he implored her to go back to her husband. She refused, saying she was very comfortable where she was, and that Byron had told her again and again that he wished she were his for life.

In despair Byron sent a note to her husband, begging him to come and take his erring wife home. Dr. Pedley's reply to the note was to send his wife's clothes and jewelry after her, with the curt message that he was done with the woman. As a compromise, Byron let Mrs. Pedley travel with him as far as London, where he proceeded to desert her.

Returning to England, Byron hawked the manuscript of "Childe Harold"—at which he had worked during his tour—from publisher to publisher. It was rejected, until Murray, of Fleet Street, decided to take a chance by printing it. On this and some other work Murray and Byron later divided profits of more than one hundred thousand dollars.

"Childe Harold" took the world by storm. Byron, to use his own phrase, "awoke one morning to find himself famous." He was the social and literary hero of the day. And to enhance this glamour, he wrapped himself the more closely in his cloak of mysterious melancholy. At dinner-parties he would not eat a mouthful. Then he would slip around to some obscure tavern, later in the evening, and would there gorge two pounds of steak.

Women found this melancholy pose irresistible. Nowadays they would probably have nicknamed him "Gloomy Gus" and steered clear of him. But they were a sentimental lot, those early-nineteenth-century damsels.

While he was still the god of the London season, Byron met Lady Caroline Lamb, peeress in her own right, and wife of the Honorable William Lamb who was afterward Lord Melbourne, Queen Victoria's first prime minister. And here began the most picturesque and violent of the poet's affairs.

LADY CAROLINE was glowingly beautiful, and she was so eccentric that as a girl her sanity had been questioned. She was a rare blend of beauty and undisciplined deviltry. At her own wedding she had burst into a fury of blasphemy against the bishop who was performing the ceremony, had ripped her wedding-dress to shreds and had been carried out of the church in screeching hysterics.

"I am dying to meet this strange Byron," she confided to rough old Samuel Rogers.

"He'll disgust you," retorted Rogers. "He bites his nails and—"

"Introduce him to me!" she commanded.

It was a case of love at first sight. From the start, Lady Caroline made no secret of her adoration for Byron. When he went to dinners or other functions to which she was not invited, she waited, openly, in the street, for him to come out. She insisted that her husband knew all about the intrigue and that he let it go on.

But if her husband was complacent, her mother-in-law was not. The old lady interfered most vehemently and whisked Lady Caroline off to Ireland. Byron, who was tiring of the impetuous beauty, used this as an excuse to break off the affair. He wrote to Caroline the following chivalric letter:

> I am no longer your lover. Since you oblige me to confess it by this truly unfeminine persecution, learn that I am attached to another..... As a last proof of my regard, I offer you this advice: Correct your vanity, which is ridiculous. Exert your absurd caprices on others; and leave me in peace.

On receipt of this letter, Caroline went wild with rage. She burned Byron in effigy, at Brocket Park, Dublin. And she hired a band of girls to dance around the "funeral pyre," clad in white and chanting a death-song. After this Caroline took to drinking brandy mixed with laudanum, and she publicly insulted Byron, every time she met him.

The next was a woman of forty—Lady Oxford, of whose "glorious autumnal charms" Byron sang. But presently he formed a new attachment and forgot her.

PRESENTLY Byron decided to marry and settle down. He chose as a wife Isabelle Milbanke—the last woman on earth he should have married. He proposed to her. She rejected him. He was overjoyed at his escape. But Miss Milbanke would not let him go so easily. She managed to ensnare him and induce him to marry her. He never forgave her for this, and he set out to make her life a burden. He succeeded.

She was a catty, narrow-minded woman, presumably virtuous, but with the soul of a flea. On their wedding-day she told him she had married him to reform him.

"Many are the tears you will have to shed," he sneered, "before you succeed in doing that. Meanwhile, it is enough for me to hate you."

Their nuptial life, thus auspiciously begun, went from bad to worse. Soon Lady Byron demanded a separation. She would not free her husband by divorce, but she would not live with him any longer.

As a parting sting she made charges against him that smashed his reputation and drove him forever from England. These charges cannot be quoted here. Harriet Beecher Stowe wrote them out—even quoting Lady Byron's own bald language concerning them—in a magazine of which Mrs. Stowe was editor. And she lost her editorial job by doing so. This article by Mrs. Stowe was reprinted in England,—in Macmillan's Magazine for 1869,—where it roused a whirlwind of discussion.

Whether or not Lady Byron's accusations were true, I don't know. Nobody knows. They have been vigorously denied, and there is no shadow of proof that they were anything more than the outpouring of the venom in an angry and nasty woman's heart. But they were of a kind that called for no proof. The mere statement of them was enough, at the time, to make Byron an outcast from his native land.

Of course he capitalized the subject by writing a poem about it, which he afterward sold at a big price and which you have perhaps read. It was addressed to his wife, and it began:

> Fare thee well! And if forever,
> Then forever fare thee well!

He sent a manuscript copy of it to Lady Byron in hope of softening her wrath toward him. But he also inclosed in the same letter the weekly butcher-bill. And on the back of the poem he scrawled the loving words:

> I'm quite certain we never ate as much meat as all that, in one week.

This, in its way, was as truly Byronic as his earlier remark about Coburn's wine. His mind, as well as his verse, was a blend of divine beauty and of ludicrously sordid matter of fact.

A protracted love-affair with Claire Clairmont, the Drury Lane actress, did not lighten his heart or ease the rebuffs that everywhere met him. He was down and out financially, and for a time he was almost a dead beat. One biographer thus describes him at this dark period:

> He sank into a lounger—shabby, fat, yellow, unshaven, loafing in one club or another, begging and borrowing.

Presently the strain grew too tense. Byron left England—driven away by a spiteful woman's unproved assertions. He went to Italy.

THITHER Claire Clairmont (her original name, it is said, was Jane Something-or-other) went also. Though he soon tired of her, she adored him to the day of her death. Long years after his body was dust, she wrote this terse account of the romance:

The Woman Tamers

I was overwhelmed. The great Lord Byron loved me. Nothing else mattered.

In Italy and Switzerland the exile found a veritable mob of new loves. He even laid lazy siege to the affections of "the most gorgeous Lady Blessington." The Lady afterward said the siege had been in vain; and she ought to have known. But he managed to sell his leaky old yacht to Lady Blessington's husband for an enormous sum, and so the courtship was not wholly unprofitable to him.

He was more fortunate—artistically though not financially—in his suit for the love of a dashing Irish girl, Eliza Oliver. After he left Miss Oliver, their daughter was born. This daughter was known to fame as Lola Montez—the superwoman who kicked the Bavarian throne to matchwood, and who boasted loudly of her Byronic origin. Lola Montez, by the way, is buried in Greenwood Cemetery, Brooklyn, her battered little tombstone bearing the name *Eliza Gilbert*.

It was during this loitering trip through Italy and Switzerland that Byron met the last and worthiest love of his life, the Countess Guiccioli. She made a man of him, as nearly as nature and his vanity would let her. She gave him a new interest in living.

Here, too, Byron met Percy Bysshe Shelley—soul of fire in a body of fragile glass—and Shelley's wife. Together the four wandered through Italy. Shelley wrote, of the Countess:

> She is a very pretty and sentimental Italian lady. If I know anything of Byron, she will have plenty of time and opportunity to repent her rashness in loving him.

Byron longed to marry the Countess, but Lady Byron stubbornly refused to divorce him. So matters went on, without benefit of clergy.

Soon Shelley died. Byron and Trelawney and other friends of the dead genius cremated him. The funeral pyre was built on the seashore. Whenever emotion or smoke proved too strong, Byron would jump into the sea for a swim, coming back refreshed to witness the burning.

SOON afterward Byron went to Greece, where a revolution against the Turks had begun. Byron now chose to regard himself as a noble patriot. He wrote stirring poems on Greek liberty and vowed to lay down his life on the altar of Grecian independence.

He spent so much time posing as a revolutionary hero that he had no time left for fighting. While the hottest battles for Greek freedom were waging, Byron loafed at Missolonghi, writing poetry, swimming, and flirting with dark-eyed peasant girls.

There a fever seized him—brought on partly by the climate and partly by his efforts to keep down his flesh by sousing his food in vinegar. The news of his illness thrilled all Greece. Throughout Europe went word that the poet-patriot was losing his life for the holy cause of liberty. With feeble hand Byron wrote his own swan-song:

> My days are in the yellow leaf;
> The flowers and fruits of love are gone.
> The worm, the canker and the grief
> Are mine alone!

He died on April 19, 1824—having crowded into thirty-six hectic years the work of a long lifetime and the loves of a dozen lives. As he lay dying—either delirious or pretending to be—he fancied himself upon the field of battle (where he had never been) and shouted fiercely:

"Forward! Forward! Courage! Follow me! Don't be afraid! Forward!"

Later his eyes opened. Seeing one of his friends of the Italian days leaning over his bed, he whispered:

"Don't grill me, as we did poor Shelley!"

II — Napoleon Bonaparte
Conqueror of Thrones and Women

"ONLY one woman has ever loved me. No, she was not my mother. And assuredly she was not my wife. She was my old nurse."

That was Napoleon Bonaparte's bitter summing up of his hundred love-affairs. Grossly fat, and chattering like a magpie instead of bearing himself as a "caged eagle" might reasonably be supposed to, he sat in his St. Helena prison, with death drawing near. With a clear vision he looked back over his affairs with all types of women. And that was his grim epitome of it all.

Yet in his days of greatness, no woman had been able to withstand him. Women as well as men looked on him as a god. The only woman to whom he gave his heart was faithless and made fun of him; but there were dozens more to console him for her loss.

This is the story of Napoleon the Lover, not of Napoleon the History-Maker. It begins when the eighteen-year-old Corsican lieutenant—shy, homely, awkward, penniless—wandered through the streets of Paris at night, bitterly lonely.

He could not make friends with his brother-officers. They laughed at his rough foreign accent (an accent he could never get rid of as long as he lived) and at his screeching rages and they despised his queer moods and his down-at-heel poverty. He in turn made no secret at all of the fact that he looked on them as a parcel of empty-headed snobs. Nor was there other society in the French capital with which the solitary boy could mingle. So, during the evenings when he was not on duty, he took to roaming the streets.

There, one night, he met a girl of his own age—a girl whose real name he probably never knew. She belonged to the oldest profession on earth. She had been driven to it when the soldier-sweetheart who brought her to Paris from her country home deserted her. The lonely girl and the lonely boy were drawn to each other by the very ties of solitude and penury and stranger-hood which repelled the rest of the world from them. An odd romance began, more idealistic than vulgar; and it went on for the best part of a year. Then the girl vanished, leaving the young Corsican more alone in the world than ever. He tells the whole story in one of his queerly reminiscent letters.

Then Napoleon met Caroline de Colombier, at whose father's house he was a barely tolerated visitor. And a second romance set in—a romance as idealistic as the first, but with no trace of sordidness, a pretty boy-and-girl love-affair. The young people used to gather cherries in the Colombier garden and recite poetry to each other and plan a truly golden future. But this lasted a pitiably short time. The Colombiers had no intention of throwing away their daughter on an impecunious foreigner who had no future or friends. So they married Caroline to a well-to-do retired officer many years older than she. His name was Garempil de Brissieux.

The Colombiers thought it a fine match. For the man could not only support a wife in comfort, but he was actually a member of the petty nobility. They engineered the marriage to a triumphal climax—thereby losing the opportunity of seeing their beloved daughter crowned Empress of France. Napoleon always had the sweetest memories of Caroline. Long afterward, when he was emperor, he heard she was living in poverty, at Lyons. He went to Lyons to visit her, gave a lucrative job to her impoverished husband, made him a baron, promoted her brother in the army and established Caroline herself as a lady-in-waiting.

Soon after Caroline's marriage, Napoleon fell in love with Mlle. Lamberie de St. Germain. She rejected him for her cousin, a richer man. In after years, Napoleon crowded honors and wealth on the couple. He told her husband:

"I once loved your wife. I loved her for her goodness as much as for her beauty."

THIS brings to an end the list of such love-affairs of Napoleon's as savored of lavender and marriage-bells. The rest were less proper if far more interesting. I have cited these early romances to show that his power over women did not begin until the beginning of his hypnotic power over men and over dynasties. There were other equally mild and less worthy intrigues dotted through his days of poverty, but none really worth the mentioning.

The French Revolution came and went, to be followed by the wildly corrupt days of the Directorate. After years of tragedy and gloom, Paris blossomed out in mad gayety. "Here, and at this time, alone of all the places in the world," writes a historian, "woman found her empire and her true power. Nor were the women of this era in their first youth. The most fascinating of them were from thirty to forty years old."

France was ruled by a committee known as the Directors. And the Directors, in turn, were ruled by such women as these. It was a sorry period enough, so far as morals and statesmanship went. But it was decidedly jolly for everyone concerned, even for Napoleon Bonaparte.

With patched boots and faded uniform, the lonely young Corsican strode through the salons of these gorgeous women of the Directorate. He himself, though barely past the mid-twenties, was now a general; and he was a protégé of Barras, the most powerful and most corrupt of the Directors.

Barras, sometime before, had fallen in love with a daintily graceful and charming Creole widow, Josephine Beauharnais. She had beauty, of an early-fading sort. She had no brains, no education, no morals, and (beyond a careless good-nature) no good traits at all. She had been grossly and openly unfaithful to her husband; her affairs could be numbered by the score. And now, in the heyday of French official corruption, she ruled as the acknowledged favorite of Barras.

But Josephine was getting along in years, for a Creole. Her dark skin was sallowing. Wrinkles were creeping around her eyes. Her teeth were beginning to decay and to turn brown. There were younger and lovelier women maneuvering to take her place. Barras was becoming tired of her, and he was looking for a chance to get rid of her. His chance soon came, and he took it.

Napoleon chanced to meet Josephine. He met her again, at a reception at Barras' house. He fell crazily in love with her. He must have known what the woman's past had been and what she then was, but he was too blindly adoring to care. He behaved like an impetuous schoolboy—besought her to marry him and followed her everywhere. It was the one time in all his selfishly crafty life that his heart ran away with his head.

NOW, Josephine cared not the snap of her fingers for the awkwardly worshiping Corsican. She did not pretend to. Indeed, she was in love with a poor officer named Hippolyte Charles. But she had sense enough to know she was growing old and that she was losing her grip on Barras. She went to Barras for advice, and Barras saw his opportunity to free himself from her.

He told her Napoleon had a great future and advised her to marry the Corsican. He also promised to give Napoleon, as a wedding-present, the command of France's ragged Army of Italy and to advance (presumably from the public funds) any needful cash.

Josephine accepted these terms, and with them Napoleon's offer. She lied about her age, knocking several years off of it, in making her wedding-deposition to the notary. And on November 8, 1796, she and Bonaparte were married. Barras and Tallien (both of whom had been her lovers) were the official witnesses to the ceremony.

Two days later Napoleon set off to join his army and to turn it from a disorganized mob into the most terrible fighting-machine in all Europe. He entreated Josephine to go to Italy with him. She was having far too good a time in Paris, and she refused. Now that she was legally married, she at last had a definite position in society. Married to a general, she also had credit and could spend money she did not own. All this was far better than to tramp over Italy with an army. So she stayed where she was; and Napoleon was still so madly in love that he let her do as she chose. To Italy he went and to the first step in immortal military fame. Josephine remained in Paris, spending money and living openly with Hippolyte Charles.

Letters are stupid reading, at best, except to the person who writes or receives them. But I am going to quote one or two passages, if you will try not to skip them, from Napoleon's twice-a-day letters to Josephine during this Italian campaign. He kept couriers busy riding to Paris with these letters. They are worth reading. When you recall that he never cared for any other woman and that the one woman to whom he thus bared his adoring soul was deceiving him with another man, they take on a certain pathos of their own:

"When I am tempted to curse my fate," begins one of his letters, "I lay my hand over my heart and touch your picture that lies there. Then my love for you makes me gloriously happy again; and all life seems golden, except the black time I must spend away from you."

The "picture" of which he wrote was Josephine's miniature. He wore it next his heart. Staff officers, entering his tent suddenly one night, found him praying to it as if before an altar.

Again he wrote: "Oh, my darling, you are coming to me, aren't you? You will soon be here, where I can clasp you close to the heart that beats for you alone. Take wings, sweetheart, and fly to me!"

But Josephine yawned as she read the burning appeal. Then she went to the theater with Charles.

WHEN Napoleon grew more insistent in his demands that she join him, she wrote a lie as to her physical condition—a lie that made her husband drunk with happiness and stopped his entreaties that she risk the rough journey over the Alps. Henceforth his one wish was to get back to Paris to her. To get back, he must first conquer Italy. So he threw himself into the campaign with a fury that carried everything before it.

An immortal opera-singer at Milan—Grassini, one of the most beautiful women of her day—made fervid love to Napoleon. He laughed in her face and then turned his back on her. Loving Josephine as he did, all other women were as shadows to him.

Meantime, Josephine's conduct was shocking even the society of easy-going Paris. Scared into propriety, she consented at last to join her husband in Italy. By this time Napoleon had Italy under his feet. He was the hero of the day, the all-conqueror. Everybody clamored to do honor to his wife. Gifts and bribes were showered upon the dazzled Josephine, who began vaguely to realize that she had married a man of some importance. He could refuse her nothing. So she wheedled military and state secrets from him and peddled them to his enemies, thus reaping a very tidy bit of pin-money.

But when Napoleon went to conquer Egypt, she flatly refused to leave Paris for so barbarous a country. He left her behind, and at once she went back to her old loose life. This time, members of Napoleon's family wrote to him, telling him some plain truths about his wife and adding the information that several of his generals knew all about her conduct. Napoleon sent for General Lefèbre and demanded:

"What is Josephine doing at this moment?"

"Weeping for your return," was the general's dutiful reply.

"You lie," courteously retorted Napoleon. "She is riding in the Bois, and with the worst company she can find. Now tell me what you know."

Thus adjured, Lefèbre told. And Napoleon, in a maniac fury of jealousy, deserted his army and boarded the fastest France-bound ship he could find.

News of her husband's approach was sent to Josephine. In guilty terror she set forth to meet him. She took the wrong road—no novelty in her frail and silly life—and missed him. When she turned back to Paris, Napoleon was already there. And he had heard some interesting additions to his earlier news of her. Incidentally he had had Charles arrested and sent to prison.

The frightened woman hurried to her house. Napoleon would not let her in. She pounded her stupid head against the door and wept. Her son and daughter—by her first marriage—joined her there. They also wept; the servants wept; everybody wept.

Finally, Napoleon, who had a grim sense of humor, unbarred the door and bade them all come in and stop making blubbering fools of themselves. He took Josephine back as his wife, but his love was dead. He now saw her for what she was, and he treated her, henceforth, with tolerant civility.

Worthless as Josephine had been, she had brought him luck. His marriage to her had given him his first real chance as an army leader. His eagerness to get back to her had helped him win his whirlwind Italian campaigns. Now, his sudden return from Egypt landed him in the very middle of a political crisis in which his timely presence enabled him to make himself master of all France.

NOW that his eyes were opened and his love was dead, Napoleon promptly made up for lost time by seeking to win new hearts. And as he was the idol of the whole country, he found such conquests ridiculously easy. Women who once would not have looked at the half-starved Corsican adventurer now fawned upon him.

He paid Josephine's debts (they amounted to $1,400,000) and pretended to forget the past. Indeed, he probably did forget it. For once having lost interest in anything, he was too busy a man to revive it. I don't know whether or not she gave him further cause for jealousy. But assuredly, he was never again jealous.

The odd part of it all is that Josephine, who had never loved him, was furiously jealous of all Napoleon's many later sweethearts. She spied on him and bored him to death with hysterical reproaches. Perhaps some woman may be able to explain this bit of feminine psychology. A mere man cannot hope to.

Josephine was furiously jealous of all Napoleon's later sweethearts. She spied on him..... used to prowl about the stairways and halls outside his apartments.

You remember Grassini, the beautiful singer whom Napoleon had flouted for love of Josephine? He now sent for her to come to Paris to sing in opera there. He conducted the affair with discreet privacy. This did not suit Grassini, who knew the advertising value of a public scandal. When she found she could gain nothing in prestige from Napoleon's infatuation for her, she revenged herself by eloping with Rode, the great violinist. She went further; after Napoleon's fall, she attached herself to his arch-enemy the Duke of Wellington.

Nor was Napoleon himself above a bit of Corsican revenge. He used to punish Josephine for her infidelity by inviting actresses and opera sopranos to sup with him in his private apartments at the Tuileries, and he took care that the tearfully jealous Josephine should be told of these suppers. She used to prowl about the stairways and halls outside his apartments at such times, in an anguish of jealousy, yet not daring to break in on the revels.

He never let love interfere with business. For example, one night the renowned Mlle. Duchesnois had allowed herself to be coaxed into supping with him after the theater. Blushingly she was led into the study where Napoleon sat reading some important dispatches that had just arrived. A valet tiptoed forward to announce the fair actress' presence.

"I'm too busy to bother with her!" snarled Napoleon, not even looking up from his papers. "Give her five hundred francs and tell her to get out!"

Mlle. Georges, most noted actress of her time, caught his fancy. Napoleon, at their first meeting, glanced critically at her from head to feet—especially feet. She was gloriously handsome, but she had enormous splay feet—wearing a number seven shoe; though even that ample size pinched her.

"You have hideous feet," was Napoleon's loverly greeting. "I should hate to see them without shoes or stockings to cover them."

Yet for two years their intrigue continued—to Josephine's misery. And all the time he treated Mlle. Georges more brutally than most men would treat a dog, rewarding her slavish adoration with studied roughness.

Once she timidly begged him for a portrait of himself. Taking from his pocket a handful of coins, he selected a gold-piece known as a "Napoleon" and bearing the impress of his features on it.

"There you are!" said he, flipping it at her. "It's said to be a very good likeness, too."

She was the only one of his countless loves who remained wholeheartedly devoted to Napoleon, in good luck and in bad. To the day of her death, long years later, she worshiped and revered his memory—perhaps because he had treated her so badly, throughout.

Mme. de Vaudry, a woman of high birth and lady-in-waiting to Josephine, cut out several rivals and basked for a little while in the Emperor's favor. But she overplayed her hand. When she sent word to him by Duroc that she must give him up and leave France, unless her heavy debts were at once paid, he replied:

"I've neither money nor good-nature enough to pay such a price for what I can get more cheaply. Thank Mme. Vaudry for her many kindnesses, and never mention her name to me again."

On receipt of this message Mme. Vaudry tried to kill herself by poison. But she lived to be an old woman and died a pauper.

TO his credit, Napoleon never once sought the love of any woman whom he believed to be good. On the rare occasions when he chanced to become interested in such women, he took himself at once out of their lives, leaving them none the worse for him.

It was after he had divorced Josephine and had sought to strengthen his dynasty by marrying the cowlike Archduchess Marie Louise of Austria (who dreaded and hated him) that Napoleon visited Poland. For some reason or other, the Poles thought—as had the Irish—that he meant to liberate their oppressed country. All Poland went wild with enthusiasm over him—notably, the loveliest woman in Poland, Countess Marie Walewska. "Young, slim, blue-eyed and exquisite as a fairy," she is described.

Marie was the loveless bride of a seventy-year-old Polish nobleman. Napoleon was charmed by her. She came nearer winning his real love than had any woman except Josephine. He invited her to a ball he was giving at a palace in Warsaw. Marie knew what the invitation meant; moreover she did not believe so selfish a man as Bonaparte would do anything for her stricken country: she refused to go to the ball.

At once the foremost nobles of Poland besought her to go, in behalf of her fatherland. She went. That was how she, personally, regarded

Napoleon. To the last, or as long as a shadow of hope remained, she tried to use her influence with him for Poland's benefit. Hers was a true patriotic sacrifice, but it was in vain. Napoleon wooed her thus, brusquely:

"I have already lifted the name of your country from the dust. Remember that even as I crush this watch in my hand, so shall your country and all your hopes be crushed if you repulse my love and refuse me yours."

Needless to say, Napoleon did not free Poland. When Marie found that Napoleon's power was at an end, she deserted him.

Her desertion was a blow to Napoleon's pride as well as to his battered heart. She was the last of his long array of loves. And the news that she had repudiated him was the chief cause of his unhappy outburst:

"Only one woman has ever loved me! My old nurse!"

III — Jonathan Swift
The Great Bear of Love and Literature

"ZOO must cly Lele and Hele aden. Must loo mimitate Pdfr., pay? Iss, and so shall! and so leles fol ee rettle. Dood mollow."

Yes, you read it aright the first time. No, the fault is not with my secretary nor with the compositor nor even with the proof-reader. Neither am I, personally, trying to be funny, nor am I slumping into aphasia.

Go to any public library. Ask for the "Journal" of Jonathan Swift—Right Reverend Dean of St. Patrick's and author of "Gulliver's Travels." And therein you will find the idiotic quotation that begins this article. You will find more language of the same paretic kind.

Cranky old Dean Swift was not inventing a new language or using a cipher. He was writing baby-talk. The "Journal" was written for a woman he loved. And that is the way he used to talk to her.

Remember, please, that Swift was neither an amorous schoolboy nor an imbecile. He was not only one of the foremost writers, statesmen and orators in Europe, two hundred years ago, but he was a human grouch, as well—the most savage, satiric, ugly-tempered man of his day.

Not being a mind-reader, I cannot translate, in its entirety, the baby-talk I have just quoted. But we have Swift's own testimony that "Pdfr." is short for "Poor dear foolish rogue." "Rettle" means "letter," and "Hele and Lele" is a Swift-version of "here and there."

And now, if the foregoing idiocy has caught your attention, suppose we get on to the story.

He was born in 1667, this Irish genius, at Dublin, a month or two after his father's death. His widowed mother could not support him, and Jonathan was left to the mercy of relatives for his upbringing. It was a mercy that savored mightily of stinginess and of grudged charity. It soured the sensitive boy, even as early ill-treatment will make a dog either dangerously fierce or else cowed and spiritless. It made Swift savage and cross-grained, and he never got over it. Year by year his snarling moroseness grew worse.

Added to this setback there were physical defects that went still further to curdle his nature and to set him apart from the rest of mankind. He was homely, too—with a lanky body, a great jutting beak of a nose, and bulging blue eyes thatched by a pair of brows that looked like Alaska sable cuffs. His voice was a blend of falsetto and growl. He seldom washed or shaved.

No, there was nothing about him, in general appearance, that could make a hit with any woman. He did not even have money or—until late in life—fame. Yet he was loved as few normal men have been loved. One or two of his personal romances are numbered among the deathless love-stories of history. And it is with only the more important of his affairs that we shall deal.

The first was his courtship of Jane Waring, a pretty girl who had an income of a hundred pounds a year. Swift, at that time, had a little less than nothing. He was just starting his clerical life in a poor Irish parish, where his total congregation numbered just fifteen persons. Most of these fifteen seem to have had a lamentable habit of staying away from church. Often there was no one present at the services except Swift himself and his old sexton Roger. At such times Swift would vary the reading of the Church of England service which begins: "Dearly beloved brethren, the Scripture moveth us in sundry places, to confess, etc."

Instead, with grouchy unction, he would begin: "Dearly beloved Roger, the Scripture moveth you and me, in sundry places, etc."

Miss Waring tried to be prudent and to listen to her family's warnings that it was unwise to wed a man of Swift's nature and poverty.

So, though she loved him ardently, she suggested that they wait until the young wooer's prospects should be brighter. This was common sense. But what lover ever cared to listen to common sense? Assuredly, Jonathan Swift did not. The same traits which made Jane hesitate to marry a virtual pauper would of course have made her doubly valuable, later, as a poor clergyman's wife. But Swift did not see it that way.

Grouchily he assented to her plea for delay; and he began to work harder—apparently with the idea of earning enough to marry on. Gradually, his fortunes improved. At last he obtained a parish which paid him a salary of four hundred pounds a year. That was a splendid living wage, in an age when skilled cooks could be hired for about twenty-five dollars a year and when the best meat cost less than eight cents a pound, and when comfortable houses rented for a bare yearly hundred dollars.

Combined with Miss Waring's annual five hundred dollars, Swift's income was almost a fortune. Miss Waring herself thought so; and she wrote to Swift that she thought they might venture, now, to marry. Swift had been waiting in sneering impatience for just such a message from her. It was a moment that repaid him for the jar to his vanity and temper caused by her plea for delay. He sat down at once to answer her. Here, in part, is his letter—which Smith cites as "a peerless example of frank brutality:"

> Are you competent to manage domestic affairs with an income of less than sixty pounds a year? Will you comply with my wishes and my way of living, and endeavor to make us both as happy as you can? Will you agree to my methods for improving your mind so as to make us entertaining companions for each other?
> If you can answer these questions in the affirmative, I shall be willing to marry you, whether your face be fair or not, or your fortune large or small. Cleanliness in the first and competency in the second is all I expect from you.

Strangely enough, Jane Waring—or "Varina," as Swift called her—did not even bother to answer this loving letter; and the affair ended with great suddenness—as Swift had intended that it should.

Miss Waring lived to be grateful for her escape from the claws of such a bear. But she was perhaps the only victim of Swift to escape with so little injury to heart or to vanity.

The next was Stella. Of course, Stella was not her real name at all. She

He sat down at once to answer her. His letter was a "peerless example of frank brutality."

bore the much less poetic name of Esther Johnson. It was the custom, in that age of outward high-flown courtesy and inward bestiality, for lovers to call each other by some romantic title as different as possible from their rightful names. Witness the flirtation of one Peter Smithers and Susanna Hoffo, in Queen Anne's reign. Peter addressed Susanna as "Artemesia," while she called him "Eugenio."

Swift had a knack of his own for such nicknames. Varina surely has a prettier sound than Jane. And Stella—Latin word for star—is more flowery than plain Esther Johnson. (Esther, by the way, is Hebrew for star. So the nickname was not so farfetched, after all.)

The memory of Swift's affair started the fashion of naming girls Stella—a custom that has never wholly died out.

Esther Johnson—or let's follow her lover's example and call her Stella—was described as "a dark-haired, bright-witted beauty." She was eight years old when Swift first met her, and he was in the late twenties. Her widowed mother was a pensioned hanger-on of Sir William Temple, who was Swift's patron.

Between the gawky and cranky young clergyman and the brilliant child a tenderly sweet friendship sprang up. He acted as her tutor; and her cleverness and affection whiled away many of his own drearily lonely days.

Then he went away from Temple's house to begin his career; and when he next met Stella, she was seventeen. At once she fell in love with the sour-visaged misanthrope. When he went to London, on political duty, she used to write to him every day. Swift treasured her simple little notes, reading them till they were almost illegible, carrying them in his breast pocket all day and hiding them under his pillow at night.

He not only replied to them in kind, but he also kept a sort of diary which was also a daily news-letter to her. This he called "Stella's Journal." It is a model of literary skill and a vivid chronicle of England's court and political life. In addition it is, in spots, the most driveling idiocy ever written. For the grimly caustic Swift, whose vitriol tongue and pen were already dreaded by all London, filled page after page of the "journal" with such wishy-washy baby talk as I have already quoted.

One of his Journal entries ends with an outburst of love for Stella, accompanied by the capital letters "M. D.," repeated seven times in succession. "M. D." was his chosen abbreviation for "My Dear."

If you like that brand of slush, here is a cross-section from a Stella letter in Swift's "Journal"—a letter he wrote, propped up in bed and by the light of one guttering candle:

> Faith, to-day came a letter from my own sweet little M. D. I will not answer it, now, no-o-o-o-o, but will keep it under my pillow. Here it is, just under the pillow. Oh! I lifted up the pillow and saw it there! Yes, little letter, you shall not be answered until the morning, for I must go to sleep. I shall be expecting every day a pretty letter from my own M. D.
> See how this is all blotted! I can write no more, but tell you I love M. D. dearly. Cadenus loves his M. D. God Almighty bless and preserve my little M. D.!

Cadenus is an anagram on Decanus, Latin word for Dean, and referred to Swift's own title of Dean of St. Patrick's, in Dublin.

When Swift moved to Dublin, Stella and an elderly woman cousin came thither also and settled in a cottage a mile or so away from him. Stella presided at all the deanery's social affairs, but primly returned each night to her own home and to the old lady who was her nominal chaperon. For years, this went on, Swift yearly growing more crabbed and brutal in his behavior toward the girl, and Stella ever waxing more and more adoring of her bearlike lover.

At last she could bear her doubtful position no longer. Summoning all her courage, she begged Swift to marry her. Swift flew into a rage, declaring he would do nothing of the sort.

"Marriage," he snarled, "has many children. Among them are Repentance, Discord, Jealousy and Loathing. I want none of it."

But Stella, usually so meek and yielding, would not give up her point. She shrank tearfully away from the raging man. But as soon as he calmed down, she returned to the attack—not shrewishly or with nagging, but in the gentle and loving persistence that is woman's deadliest weapon.

Kennedy once wrote of "the Terrible Meek." And meekness is far more terrible than bluster—as Swift at last discovered. Worn down by her wordless reproach and by her gently endured grief, he finally consented to make her his wife. But though he could, at a pinch, do the right thing, he could do nothing graciously. And he saddled his growled surrender with such terms as must have humiliated the poor girl almost past endurance.

First of all, he was careful to make it very clear to Stella that this marriage was a mighty sacrifice on his part and that it was abhorrent to him. Next he made her swear to keep the union a secret forever, and not to bear his name. Third, he arranged that the ceremony should be performed at dead of night and that no record of it should be made on the cathedral archives.

Stella sobbingly agreed to all this. To punish her still further for her presumption in marrying him, Swift never again would speak to her or even enter her presence, except before witnesses.

It is not clear just what joy it was possible for the poor woman to glean from such an unavowed and empty marriage—beyond the bliss of having carried her point and gotten her way. Tragedy, moreover, was lurking not far behind, as a result of the strange wedding—tragedy, not for Stella, but for another woman.

THE "other woman" was Hester Vanhomrigh, whom Swift had met, long before, during his stay in London. Her mother was a woman of wealth and social rank. Swift was a frequent visitor at her house. He courted Hester ardently; and as usual he bestowed a nickname on her. He called her "Vanessa;" and he wrote poems about her which nowadays would have landed him in prison, for sending them through the mails, but which, in that age, passed as gallantly complimentary.

With all his bearish and boorish ardor, he devoted himself to courting Vanessa—even while writing his daily "Journal" to Stella. Vanessa had heard many a love-vow from many a Londoner of rank and charm; but love had never stirred her heart until she listened to the rough wooing of the slovenly middle-aged dean. She was the type of woman who would rather be kicked than kissed; and Swift was far more skillful at kicking than at kissing. The harshness which made gentle Stella flinch thrilled Vanessa with the delight of his mastery.

In a remarkably short time she was returning Swift's love, and returning it with compound interest. She became his madly adoring slave, his abject worshiper. His brutality made her the more hopelessly enamored of him. But as Vanessa warmed, Swift cooled. Such wholesale adoration bored him. He snubbed Vanessa. She clung the closer to him. He insulted and rebuffed her. She knelt at his feet in a rapture of love. This new semblance of aversion on his part was the one thing needed to make her his forever. Swift left London and went to Dublin to live.

Vanessa followed and took a house at a village nine miles away.

There is an impulse that makes a man tolerate and even pet and cherish a stray dog that has the good judgment to follow him home and refuse to be driven away from him. The same impulse warmed Swift's grim heart toward the woman who had given up everything for his sake and who had, unasked, followed him into exile.

Thus, the love-affair (begun and broken off in London) was renewed in Ireland. And an odd state of affairs set in.

STELLA and Vanessa were living less than ten miles apart. Neither of them had heard of the other. And Swift was constantly visiting them both. For years this went along. The grouchy old lover played his cards cleverly. He carried on two desperate love-affairs at the same time,—and with two women only nine miles apart,—yet kept each from finding out the other's existence.

Perhaps it was genius that enabled him to do this; perhaps it was only luck. (Some men have luck!) If it was genius, Swift could have made a fortune by selling the formula to married men. But all runs of luck come to an end. And even the genius of Napoleon himself at last collapsed. Rumors of Swift's secret marriage to Stella began to seep through Dublin. And in course of time the gossip reached Vanessa.

Now, Vanessa was not overclever. She was merely overmuch in love. So, instead of keeping her mouth shut or, at worst, asking Swift about the matter, she wrote directly to Stella.

The news of her lover's supposed marriage had driven Vanessa almost insane with fear and with grief. She scarcely knew what she was doing—which ignorance did not save her from paying in full the bill for her folly.

Stella received the letter and thus discovered for the first time that there was such a woman as Vanessa on earth. She sat down and wrote an answer to Vanessa—some say, telling her the whole truth. Then she took Vanessa's letter to Swift. And hell broke loose.

I think Swift, at heart, must have been a lion for courage. Just stop for a moment, if you are a man, and consider what you would have done. I think the average man, in like predicament. would sooner pull the tail of a rattlesnake or slap Jess Willard in the face than face the music to such a tune.

The Woman Tamers

Swift was neither scared nor remorseful. Instead, he went wild with wrath. Without a word to the frigid Stella, he snatched up the letter, stamped out of the house, flung himself on his horse and galloped madly to Vanessa's home. Here is the scene that followed, as described by a much abler pen than mine.

> He drew rein at the gate and rushed up the walk. Brushing aside a servant who replied to his thundrous knock at the door, he strode into the morning-room where his Vanessa sat reading.
> He drew the letter from his pocket, brandished it in front of her panic-smitten face and then hurled it down upon the table beside her—transfixing the poor creature, the while, with a terrible glare and uttering no word. Then, still with no word to her, he left the house. Nor did she again see him or receive word of him.

Vanessa, in letters to Swift, which are still preserved, had more than once declared that she would die if ever he deserted her. Whether she hinted at suicide or whether she merely meant that she would pine away—after the manner of the anemic women of her time—I do not know. But now she made good her threat. No one can say whether she literally died of a broken heart or whether poison helped along her death. But in either case she died, a week or two after that silently wrathful visit from Swift—killed, directly or indirectly, by his brutality.

It is not on record that Swift was particularly unhappy over his ill-treated sweetheart's death. Perhaps he was too busy making his peace with Stella, and trying to explain matters to her, to have any time for sorrow just then.

But when Stella in turn faded away and died, not very long afterward, he wasted much ink and paper in lauding her virtues. He who wielded a pen so facile could not now write out the tale of his grief except in stilted sentences which seem all but heartless in their long-worded phraseology.

To drown memory, he plunged into literature and politics with a renewed zest. But he was growing old, and the springs of his life and of his mighty intellect were running dry. He waxed more and more eccentric, until presently he went hopelessly insane.

After his death, when his executors were going over his effects, they chanced upon a secret drawer in his writing-table.

A knob was pressed; the drawer slid open. It contained nothing except a crumpled and tear-stained paper on which a single line was scrawled in Swift's rude handwriting. Inside the paper was a long lock of dark hair—soft and lustrous. The written line was: "Only a woman's hair!"

What woman's? Stella's? Vanessa's? Varina's? Some one's else? That is a little heart-mystery that has never been solved.

Thackeray (a rank sentimentalist who strove to make the world regard him as a cynic) writes this tiny sermon on the finding of the unknown woman's hair in Swift's desk:

> Only a woman's hair! Only love, only fidelity, only purity, innocence, beauty—only the tenderest heart in the world stricken and wounded, and passed away out of reach of pangs of hope deferred, love insulted and pitiless desertion! Only that lock of hair left—and memory and remorse for the guilty, lonely wretch shuddering over the grave of his victim.

IV — Alexandre Dumas
The Monte Cristo Heart-Breaker

THE Grégoires were the big people of Villers-Cotterets. When they gave a party, everyone in the village struggled for an invitation. In 1818 they sent out a sheaf of invitations to a lawn-fête in honor of their niece Laura, who had just come home from a Paris convent-school. There were few young people at Villers-Cotterets. To eke out the number and to make the evening more gay for their pretty daughter, the Grégoires invited every boy or girl they knew, who could claim any shadow of good breeding.

That is how swarthy little sixteen-year-old Alexandre Dumas chanced to be bidden to the party. That, too, is how he chanced to fall in love for the first of many dozen times.

He was the only son of a general's poor widow. His parents had been degraded and impoverished by Napoleon. The widow had barely enough money to keep her alive. Young Alexandre was working as errand-boy for a local attorney.

When the Grégoires' invitation arrived, the boy was in an ecstasy of joy. His mother was not. She could not bear to keep him away from the party. But he had no clothes fit to wear to such a function. She could not afford to buy him any. And his dreamy shiftlessness and extravagance had not only prevented him from amassing enough cash to buy clothes, but had made him squander every sou he had earned.

Mme. Dumas solved the problem—as mothers will. She cut down a shabby old white dress-uniform of her dead husband's and made it over for the boy. She was not a good tailor. The buckskin breeches were skin-tight. But the coat looked more like a bathrobe than anything else.

Yet the boy, whom gaudiness always attracted, was delighted with his costume. Clad in it, he set off blissfully for the party.

The instant he set eyes upon the fair Laura he lost his heart to her. She was vastly amused by his clothes and by his ardent manner, and she proceeded to make a fool of him. With true masculine vanity, he never guessed her purpose, but was certain he was making the hit of his life. Warmer and warmer became his attentions. Laura winked at a young Paris dandy who stood near, and introduced Dumas to him.

"Ah!" drawled the dandy, coolly surveying through his monocle the lad's weirdly enveloping white coat. "I see you have your first-communion frock. But where is your taper?"

The other youths laughed loudly. Dumas spun around, red and furious, to face them. The group was gathered at one end of the Grégoire lawn, alongside a fourteen-foot ditch.

"I can't afford to dress as you fops do!" he shrilled. "But I can clear that ditch in one bound. Which of you is man enough to try it after me?"

He ran at the ditch and launched his athletic young body across it. He made the leap. But as he struck the ground at the far side, there was an ominous crack and a sound of rending. The effort had been too much for the waning strength of his ancient and tight breeches. The entire seat ripped out.

A howl of mirth from the other bank of the ditch sent him scurrying off for home at top speed—his long coat-tails enacting the rôle of charity, in that they covered a multitude of sins. Weeping, he rushed to his mother for comfort. She persuaded him to put on his workaday trousers and return to the party.

Less through obedience than from a craving to feast his eyes on Laura once more, he went back. He arrived at the Grégoires' just as the dancing began. Thrusting himself between two rivals, he besought Laura to give him the first dance. Laura took one look at his bare and perspiring hands and then said coldly:

"It would ruin the back of my white dress to dance with a gloveless cavalier."

Home once more galloped Dumas, as fast as his short legs would carry him. Again he told of his troubles to his mother. She unearthed from a chest a pair of the General's buckskin gauntlets. His hands buried elbow-deep in these, Dumas ran back to the party. Again he broke through the circle around Laura and pantingly demanded her hand for the next dance. He was a good dancer, and he yearned for this chance to show off before his divinity.

But Laura by this time was tired of the teasing she had incurred through her queer conquest. She no longer found the boy amusing. He was making her ridiculous. He had already made himself so. And these be two fatal things for any swain of any age to do.

"Run away, little fellow," she bade him sharply, "and play with your marbles or your hoop. Besides, it's time for children to be in bed."

And for the third time that day Mother Dumas presently had to comfort her heartsick son. So ended his first romance—on the very day it began.

Once having known love, Dumas would not rest until he had known it again. In less than a month he had met Adèle Dalvin, a lovely blonde milliner-apprentice. He had had quite enough of patrician society. From then till his death he chose his sweethearts from women of his own or lower rank.

Adèle was one of a group of village girls that passed as respectable—and of whom Dumas writes in his memoirs:

> Every one of them had some love-affair on hand, of a more or less serious character. They all enjoyed most delightful liberty—the result, no doubt, of the confidence their parents placed in their good sense.

A rich farmer's son had lately wooed Adèle. His family had broken off the match. Adèle was disconsolate. Dumas caught her heart on the rebound—but not until he had laid desperate siege to it for twelve long months. Her parents objected to him. His own mother forbade him to meet the girl. Yet, at last he won Adèle. He was told he might call on a certain evening at the house of a friend with whom she was staying and might knock at the closed door of a little reception-room there. He thus describes what followed:

> Behind that door I found two trembling lips, two caressing arms, a heart beating against my heart—sighs and tears.
> This room was better than an ordinary room. It was a tiny summerhouse which projected into a long garden inclosed only by hedges. A passage from the room led to the garden.
> The little girl who had given herself to me, after more than a year's struggle, was so pure, so innocent, so modest, that although my love and pride were ready to reveal everything, my conscience told me that honor, and every fine feeling I

possessed, demanded that the secret be kept with the utmost care.

Whenever I came out of the blest passage that had served me in such good stead, I made my exit by a little by-street and gained the fields. From the fields I entered a park and from the park reëntered the town by the Rue de Château.

It so happened, therefore, that my mother, who was often watching in an entirely different direction, did not see me return, and not guessing my ruse, puzzled her wits in despair to know where I had come from.

At another year's end Dumas went to Paris to take a two-hundred-and-forty-dollar-a-year clerkship in a Government office. He and Adèle wrote to each other regularly for a while. Then the girl's letters ceased. Dumas—who had not bothered, at all, to be true to her—learned from his mother that Adèle was about to marry a rich old tradesman. The news made all his love for her flare up again, for a moment, in Dumas' heart. He hurried back to Villers-Cotterets. He found his sweetheart trying on a wedding-veil and a wreath of orange-blossoms.

"Adèle!" he gasped. "What does this mean?"

"It means," she made demure answer, "that I am renewing my virginity."

The reply was too much for Dumas' jealous anger. He exploded into Homeric laughter—and stayed on at Villers-Cotterets for the wedding.

It was not until 1827 that he saw or heard of Adèle again. This time it was in Paris they met. In the interval, he had begun to wax successful as a playwright. Going home, late one night, he saw several people fighting, near the Gate of St. Denis. Running up, Dumas found that two thieves had set upon a man and a woman. He struck one of the thieves with his cane, and the fellow ran away.

Just then, up came the police. They seized Dumas, the man and woman, and the remaining thief, lugged them off to the station-house and locked all four of them, for the night, in the same cell.

The woman was Adèle. With her husband, she had come to Paris to see one of Dumas' plays. On the way to their hotel from the theater the couple had been attacked by footpads. The four spent a jolly night chatting, in the cell.

In the morning they were released. Dumas bade the thief farewell. Then he took Adèle and her husband to a sumptuous breakfast at the nearest restaurant and afterward went with them to the hotel to see their two children. Thus ended the Adèle love-story.

The Woman Tamers

ON going to Paris, Dumas found it hard to live on the two hundred and forty dollars a year he earned as a Government clerk. He hated the dull duties of his job, and he performed them so badly that only gross favoritism saved him from discharge.

He looked around for some way to earn more money and at pleasanter work. He had made friends with a youth named Leuven, who had a smattering of stage-experience. The two began to write lurid melodrama. At first they scored a series of ghastly failures. Then, bit by bit, they grew more successful. At last Dumas started out on his own account as a playwright. And presently he was famous. (Between 1832 and 1845, no less than twenty plays of his were produced. Even in earlier days he wrote at least twenty more. The total literary output of his life was sixty plays and twelve hundred books and novelettes.)

His choice of so disreputable a career as playwriting cost him his Government job. His superiors had overlooked his laziness and his blunders, but an offense of this sort was too much for their patience. Dumas was fired. Not that he cared, for he was making more money in a month than the clerkship had brought him in a year.

By this time he had made a discovery which amused rather than flattered him. He had found he was irresistible to women. Swarms of them vied for his favor. He was forever in the midst of some volcanic heart-romance. Though some of these women frankly courted him in hope of theatrical preferment or for the money he threw away as fast as he made it, yet the majority of them were his adoring slaves.

When he had first moved to Paris, as a mere boy,—living in a garret and dreaming idly of fame,—his neighbor on the floor below was Marie Catherine Lebay, a young dressmaker who was separated from her husband.

She and Dumas met on the rickety stairs one day. To the lonely country-boy the Parisian woman was a revelation in daintiness and charm. She took pity on his loneliness. The two gradually became close friends, then sweethearts.

Marie Lebay is pictured as "a kindly woman—sweet, capable, religious." Dumas' whole future might have been changed if he had been able to marry her. But he was not able to. In the first place, she had an undivorced husband. In the second, a young fellow living on two hundred and forty dollars a year and with no prospects of more does not usually think with any great seriousness of marriage.

So the affair drifted along on another plane. The couple went on a honeymoon—but it was a honeymoon that had never been through the custom house. And in 1824 a son was born to them. The son was named Alexandre Dumas in honor of his unmarried father. He lived to write "Camille," "The Corsican Brothers," "The Prodigal Father," "The Clémenceau Case" and many other great plays and novels. He became known to literature as "Alexandre Dumas, Fils," and his father as "Alexandre Dumas, Pere."

Not very long after the child's birth Dumas and Marie Lebay quarreled fiercely and separated, Marie taking the boy with her. She was very bitter, for years, against her old lover; but finally she became reconciled to him. To her death she was inordinately proud of his genius.

Young Alexandre always remained on good terms with both of his separated parents. He supported his mother by his literary earnings—which, from the first, were large. And he was forever trying in somewhat priggish fashion to induce his prodigal father to lead a better life. Saqui Smith draws this clever contrast between the two men:

"The father was big-hearted, impulsive, explosive, reckless, improvident,—his heart as big as his brain,—bubbling with sympathy for all mankind, always ready to fight the battle of the oppressed and weak, spending two gold-pieces for every one he earned, giving with both hands, going through life with his hat on one side and a girl on each knee—perfect type of a reckless, happy-go-lucky, go-day-come-day Bohemian of the old school.

"The son was a pedantic, painfully respectable person, typically bourgeois, the embodiment of all the middle-class virtues and as stingy as a Normandy peasant. He was the happy possessor of a symmetrical mediocrity which ensured his complete success. He was an able analytical writer, an accomplished scholar, master of stagecraft, gifted with intuitive understanding of his public—but lacking even a single spark of his father's heaven-born genius."

It was in the dawn of his renown as a playwright that Dumas met Marie Dorval. (He was always partial to "Marie" as a name for his sweethearts.) He had just written his first great success, "Christine," a play in which Marie starred.

The Woman Tamers 45

On his way home from the theater, after the play's first night, Dumas was hailed by a beautiful woman in a cab. "Monsieur Dumas!" she called as her cab halted. "I am Marie Dorval. Don't you know me, off the stage? Come here and kiss me! What genius you have! And how well you know how to write about women!" Thus began a scandalous but

"Monsieur Dumas!" she called. "I am Marie Dorval. Don't you know me, off the stage? Come here and kiss me! What genius you have! And how well you know how to write about women!"

very happy intrigue that went on for years. There was a ludicrous side to the story, for Marie was also courted by Alfred de Vigny, the poet. De Vigny's love was platonic. Dumas' was everything except platonic.

From time to time Dumas' glorious animalism would disgust Marie. She would turn from him to the chillier privilege of listening to De Vigny's chaste poems. Then, wearying of the poet's iceberg courtship, she would flee from it to the glowing heat of Dumas' ardor.

Paris grinned. So did Dumas. He dearly loved a joke, even when he himself was its butt.

Malibran, the immortal opera-singer, next caught at his heart. But here too a bit of sardonic humor interrupted the affair. Malibran (whose first name was also "Marie") begged Dumas to show her how to fold and fasten on an Albanian turban. She said she wanted to wear one to a fancy-dress ball.

Her lover good-naturedly consented to teach her the difficult trick. He spent an entire day at it before Malibran could master the knack.

That night he went to the opera. Zucchielli, the handsome tenor, was singing Othello to Malibran's Desdemona. The tenor came on the stage wearing an Albanian turban—folded and adjusted as only Dumas and Malibran knew how to fold and adjust it. Dumas went out, between acts, and scribbled this two-word farewell to Malibran:

"Good-by, Marie."

PRESENTLY Dumas began to write novels as well as plays. Each day, sick or well, he shut himself up in a candle-lighted room and wrote. He made it a fixed rule to cover a certain number of pages before he stopped.

Thus one day in 1844 he finished writing "The Three Guardsmen." Half a page of his daily stint remained unwritten. So, drawing a line across the middle of the page, he wrote, just below, the words:

"MONTE CRISTO—a novel, by ALEXANDRE DUMAS."

And the first few paragraphs of "Monte Cristo" were written on the same sheet as the last page of "The Three Guardsmen."

From his plays and his novels Dumas was now earning fifty thousand dollars a year—an unheard-of fortune, for a writer, in those days. But he was not content. He could not devise plots and write them out in full, fast enough to suit him. He hired a staff of hack-writers to write synopses and skeletonized novels and plays, which he elaborated and into whose dry bones he infused life.

He was the most popular author in Europe. Publishers and managers clamored for a chance to produce his work. He fed them these hack-written books and plays. Then, when the demand was not yet satisfied, he sold work of which he himself had written scarce a word.

"Have you read my latest book?" he once asked his son.

"No sir," replied the younger man. "Have you?"

Money poured in. It poured out just as fast. Dumas built for himself a wonderful castle which he called "Monte Cristo." There he lived with dozens of parasites and flatterers and hangers-on, who bled him unmercifully. He knew he could always make money. So he did not care how he spent it.

Women adored him more than ever, now that he was world-famous. And he accepted their worship as his just due. Davidson says, of this phase:

> The feminine atmosphere, the presence of women, became a necessary part of Dumas' life. Not, unfortunately, the same woman, nor yet the better sort of woman, but a succession of more or less sketchy ladies, each of whom had her day and hour and was then supplanted by another.
>
> Had Dumas been an Oriental potentate or a patriarch of ancient Israel or a Mormon of modern times, he might at fancy have added a fresh face to the collection without disturbance. Under existing conditions, all he could do was to dethrone one queen before enthroning the next. But whichever of them came or went, the type was always the same. It was always that of the mistress whose normal object is to please and flatter and get as much out of it as she can.
>
> Dumas was not a mere vulgar pursuer of women. He was always deeply in love with the lady of the moment. She was adored as well as adorable. The attachment was sentimental quite as much as sensual. It was necessary for him to feel that the woman was an inferior—a complement (in his view) and a seasoning of man—a creature who ought to be fascinating but not talented. Therefore the higher types of feminine character and intellect were not those which influenced him.

IT was at the first zenith of his repute as a playwright that Dumas met Ida Ferrier. She was an actress of very mediocre talent—short, plump, fair. She threw herself at Dumas' head. And as usual, he did not duck. Her hands and neck were her chief beauties. Dumas wrote of them:

"What shall I say of your hands? Adorable! Your neck is as white and exquisitely rounded as a swan's. Your shoulders are divine."

Ida returned his love. She spent his money almost as fast as he could earn it. He and she were seen together everywhere. He foisted her services upon unwilling managers, as the necessary condition to their producing his best plays. At last came the climax.

One evening Dumas was invited to a reception given by the Duke of Orleans, who was his patron, and in whose august esteem he strove to stand especially high.

Dumas went to the reception, and he took Ida Ferrier along. Ida, of course, had not been invited. It was no place for a woman of her sort. The Duke knew all about the affair, but in his own salon he chose to ignore the knowledge. Walking forward to greet Dumas, he turned an unrecognizing but polite gaze upon Ida and inquired:

"This is your wife, Alexandre? But I need not ask. You would not insult us by bringing an unworthy companion here."

Dumas took the hint. Next day, to the frantic disgust of his son, he and Ida Ferrier were married.

They went to live at 22 Rue de Rivoli. And for nearly four years they remained together. Long before the end of that time Ida ceased to bother about controlling her nagging and bullying temper. When life with her became unendurable, Dumas calmly told her there was to be a separation. And in spite of her scared repentance and tearful pleas for pardon, he dismissed her with a pension of twelve thousand dollars a year.

"I'll let a sweetheart make me miserable," explained Dumas in a letter to a friend. "But not a wife!"

The Woman-Tamer was getting along in years. His money-making powers were dwindling. He kept all his cash—in gold-pieces—in a big unlocked drawer in his castle, so that he or any guest or servant could help himself. But now the drawer was always empty. Nor could it be filled as easily as of yore.

People were tiring of Dumas books and plays that Dumas had not written. He wanted money. So, after he had sold his castle and everything else, he began to capitalize his fame. He peddled the use of his name in recommendation of patent medicines and the like. He wrote signed advertisements, boosting various kinds of merchandise, etc.

He even appeared as a human advertisement in a shop-window. (His son, according to the story, saw him thus and entered the shop, thrashed the proprietor and yanked his prodigal father out of the show window by the collar.)

Adah Isaacs Menken, the American adventuress, fell in love with Dumas. An enterprising camera-sharp asked leave to photograph the couple together, and offered a big sum for the privilege.

Dumas readily consented. The picture was taken. (I have seen a copy of it.) It represents Adah Menken sitting in Dumas' lap with her arms around his neck. Neither of them is in court costume.

This photograph was on sale all over Paris until Dumas' son bought up all the copies he could lay hands on and bought and destroyed the negative.

At last, in the early winter of 1870, came the end. Dead broke, forsaken by the horde of women who had fawned upon him, Dumas lay sick unto death at Puys, a suburb of Dieppe. With him was his son—from whom, almost to the end, the old man had hidden the fact of his utter poverty.

The dying genius had lain for hours in a stupor. Suddenly he opened his big black eyes and feebly asked:

"Will my follies be forgiven, boy? Will my work live after me?"

"Be at peace!" softly answered his son. "The pillar is well built. The base will stand firm."

France, at that moment, was writhing helplessly in the grip of the German invasion—a tragedy against which Dumas, again and again, had warned his fellow-Frenchmen. But the news of the great author's death almost cast into the shade the horror of the national catastrophe. All France mourned him.

The Prussian garrison at Dieppe half-masted its flags in respect to a genius whose fame belongs to no one land, but to all the world.

Maurice de Saxe, Marshal of France and one of the hundred and sixty-three children of King Augustus of Poland.

V — Marshal Saxe

The Swashbuckling Heart-Breaker

THIS is the story of a German who was the idol of France. He was Maurice, Comte de Saxe, the offspring of a churchless union between a German countess and Augustus the Strong, the German King of Poland.

(I think the title "Father of His Country" must have been first used for Augustus the Strong. Anyhow, it fitted him like a glove. For he had one hundred and sixty-three children—a tidy record, even in those ante-race-suicide days.)

Saxe was a dime-novel hero—a giant, a swashbuckler, a knight of old, born too late; and he had the gift of making himself adored by every woman who ever met him.

From boyhood, he was forever tumbling out of one adventure, into another. Once, for instance, as a lad, he and twenty of his soldiers defended a stone inn for two days against a regiment of eight hundred Poles—beating back the enemy's attacks by sheer courage and strategic skill until relief came.

From boyhood, too, he was forever getting himself into trouble of every sort, from dueling to flirtations. His royal father nicknamed him "The Firebrand." He spent fortunes he did not possess—then got his parents to finance him afresh. He was in the thick of every fight, the prize a hundred women strove for. He was magnificently handsome, built like a Colossus, and so strong that he could take the heaviest horseshoe between thumb and forefinger and crush it. He was afraid of nothing; he was true to no one. And he was a born military genius.

His father tried to make Saxe settle down by marrying him, in 1714 (when the lad was only twenty) to one of the numberless women who worshiped him—the pretty young Victoria, Countess von Loeben, an heiress.

From the first, Saxe and Victoria fought like two juvenile wild-cats.

Saxe spent his wife's fortune with both hands, and flirted brazenly with every other woman who flung herself at his head. Victoria quickly learned that it is safer to coquette with a woman-tamer than to marry one.

One day as Saxe was walking with his father in the palace park, Victoria rushed up to the King, flung herself on the ground before him and poured out the dramatic story of her grievances against her husband. She wept loudly as she told how her fortune had been squandered and she herself neglected and ill-treated, and of the scores of women who were supplanting her with Saxe.

The King gently raised Victoria from the ground. She put her arms about the royal neck, buried her face in the royal shirt-front and went on with the tearful tale of her husband's misdeeds—entreating His Majesty to punish his wayward son for such behavior toward a perfectly good wife.

The King listened in deep sympathy, petting and soothing his sobbing daughter-in-law, while Saxe stood by unconcernedly watching the scene.

"Justice shall be granted you, my poor child," declared the King at last, glancing tenderly down upon the head still pillowed on his breast.

Then, holding her close, he turned upon Saxe. In a voice of thunder he denounced the young husband, threatening to have him thrown into the darkest of dungeons for life if he did not mend his evil ways. Especially strong was the King in his rebuke of Saxe's morals. So fierce was the tirade that presently Victoria lifted her face from its refuge among the shirt-frills to beg His Majesty to show less terrific severity toward the culprit.

As she did so she caught the King winking merrily at the grinning son whom he was so mercilessly browbeating. Old Augustus the Strong was marvelously human—as his census-record shows.

That ended Victoria's last effort at reconciliation with her spouse. Henceforth it was war between them. Saxe found married life unbearable. He found also—or affected to find—that Victoria was beginning to show a more than neighborly interest in a young Italian courtier who bore the Shakespearean cognomen of Iago. Saxe brought suit for divorce.

"Aren't you content with robbing her of her fortune and her

The Woman Tamers

One day as Saxe was walking with his father in the palace park, Victoria rushed up to the King, flung herself on the path before him and poured out the dramatic story of her grievances against her husband.

happiness," demanded the King's blunt old chancellor Flemming, "without robbing her of her good name too?"

The King, who had recently quarreled with one of his own royal favorites (and had had her locked up in the prison-convent of Quedlinburg), was not in a good humor when Saxe brought to him the plea for divorce. He was still less sweet-tempered when Saxe coupled that plea with a fierce complaint about the way the royal army was mismanaged. In a burst of rage Augustus howled to his son to leave the room.

"Where shall I go?" sneered Saxe. "You can't very well send me to Quedlinburg Convent, can you?"

"No!" yelled the King. "But I can lock you in a cell under Königstein Castle, and I shall."

In dread of arrest Saxe got out of the way at top speed. There was no safe hiding-place for him except in his wife's rooms. Surely, Augustus would never think of looking there for him! But after a week in Victoria's turbulent society Saxe declared loudly:

"Death would be better than this!"

So he gave himself up. But the King's wrath had had time to simmer down, and he grudgingly forgave the sinner. The divorce matter, too, was comfortably arranged by letting Victoria do the divorcing. It is pleasant to be able to say that Victoria married a wealthy Baron von Runkel with whom she lived contentedly enough. Two of her sons and von Runkel's served under Saxe, years afterward, in France's wars.

SAXE was overjoyed at his freedom. His seven years of wedded life had given him such a horror of matrimony that he never would confess, to strangers, that he had been a husband.

"Why have you never married?" Mme. de Pompadour asked him, years later, in France.

"Madame," replied Saxe gravely, "because there are few men or women of whom I would wish to be the father, and still fewer women whom I would wish to call wife. Besides, why should I burden myself with a wife when so many of my friends have obligingly saved me the trouble?"

Sick not only of matrimony but of home and father as well, Saxe begged leave to turn his back on old scenes and to seek his fortune at Paris. The King loved his wild son and was loath to lose him. But Flemming decided the matter by saying:

"Sire, the highest service your Majesty can render your country and people is to permit the Comte de Saxe to depart for all time."

So to Paris went the young giant, taking along all the money he could raise from the sale of his local estates, and all he could wheedle his father and mother into giving him. He bought a colonelcy in a French cavalry regiment and a big house on the Quai des Théatins.

On susceptible Paris burst Maurice de Saxe like a thunderbolt, dazzling and amazing all beholders. He was a type in which the French delighted. The fame of his hero-exploits in war and in single combat had preceded him. So had the tale of his prowess with women. His beauty, his dash, his courage, his splendid strength, his prodigality with money—all these scored heavily in his favor. He became the lion of the hour, the "Man on Horseback," in short, the fashion.

Old Louis XIV of France was dead. The new king, Louis XV, was still a child. France was governed by Duke Philippe, as regent. And Philippe was living in such a way as to make the regency period a horror to all decent people.

Foremost among the court beauties was the Princesse de Conti. She had a husband who was not only a prince but a hunchback, and who was madly jealous of her. He and she were cousins. Saxe met the Princess almost directly after his arrival in Paris. She fell hopelessly in love with him. Saxe, in his spicy autobiography, says of the affair:

"It was a little conjugal comedy in the true style of the regency. In it, I played the rôle of hero—or villain, whichever you prefer. She was more lovely than the sun—gold-chestnut of hair, violet-black of eye, dazzling of skin, with the throat of a nymph. Hebelike hands, the foot of Diana and the spirit of all the Bourbons."

From which mild account one may infer that Saxe found her more or less easy to look at.

She made no secret of her love for Saxe—except to her blackly jealous husband. When the Prince accused her of having affairs with other men, she looked meaningly at his humped shoulders and replied:

"It is my consolation for having been beguiled into marrying you. Yes, I find other men interesting. There are six different ways in which I might blind you to what is going on. I will describe all six ways to you, if you like. But there is a seventh method too. I won't tell you what that is, because the seventh is the one I use."

The "seventh" (she confided to Saxe, who cynically repeated it in his autobiography) was to make Conti think she was guilty at such rare times as she really was innocent, "and thus to provoke him to some act of brutality which would justify her in leaving him."

Saxe suggested an improvement on her seventh method. He bought her a watchdog—a dog, he told the Prince, that would bark only at sight of a stranger. Conti insisted on having the guardian dog sleep just inside the Princess' private apartments. (Saxe was not "a stranger." The Prince seems to have overlooked that subtly vital point.)

One night, purposely teased into anger by the Princess, the dog broke into a paroxysm of loud barking. Conti (who spent most of his nights listening outside his wife's door) broke the door down and rushed in, brandishing a drawn sword.

Naturally, no man was to be found hiding there. The virtuously indignant Princess called in her servants to witness the outrage. Next day she left the Prince for good (or evil) and all. After that, she and Saxe were inseparable.

Saxe, meantime, was justifying the reputation he had brought with him to Paris. He drilled his regiment along lines of his own, and presently it became the best regiment in the French army. His original and brilliant ideas on warfare also won swift promotion for him.

Philippe, the regent, welcomed him gladly as a boon companion and used to invite him to the little midnight suppers at Versailles. At one of these suppers the Comtesse de Sabran made brazen love to Saxe. He was still enamored of the Princesse de Conti, and so he yawned in the Countess' face. She, by way of repartee, broke a priceless vase over his head. He carried the scar to his death-day.

Saxe's autobiography gives a brilliant—not to say lurid—account of Philippe's suppers, but I shall not repeat it, here. It wouldn't be mailable.

I AM going to skip a long chronicle of Saxe's intrigues and come at once to the real romance of his life—the affair with Adrienne Lecouvreur. Adrienne was the foremost actress alive. She was the idol of Paris. She was also a woman of great heart and intellect and of exquisite refinement. Why she should have thrown her life's love at the swaggering feet of Maurice de Saxe no one knows. For since an unhappy love-story in earlier days, she had been deaf to all men's entreaties.

Saxe, long after Adrienne's death, wrote patronizingly of her as his "guardian angel." While she lived, he treated her abominably. He quickly fell under her influence, and he let her mold his roughness into something like elegance. Says Lemonty:

> Saxe learned from the glorious Adrienne everything except war—which he already knew better than anyone else did—and spelling—which he never knew at all.

Adrienne looked on him as a Homeric hero. She worshiped him. At first, amazed at her elusive charm, he returned her adoration. Gradually he grew content to let her worship him, and to repay her in any way he chose.

She made him become a naturalized Frenchman; she taught him diplomacy and manners; she coached him in ways to improve his position at court. Patiently she endured his many infidelities and his occasional fits of jealous bad temper.

Then came Saxe's great chance. And it was Adrienne who showed him how to use it—even though she knew it must separate him from her. Her love was above all selfishness. The chance was this:

The throne of the Russian duchy of Courland had become vacant. Saxe entered a claim for nomination as duke. Money was needed for bribes and for the many other expenses connected with the venture, and Saxe, as usual, had no money. He wrote to his mother, who at once sold all her plate and jewelry and sent him the proceeds. But it was not enough. So Adrienne Lecouvreur sold all her own jewels, her house and everything she owned, and mortgaged her future salary as an actress. In this way she raised one hundred and fifty thousand dollars. All of it she turned over to Saxe.

Thus financed by two women, Saxe set forth for Courland. And here again a woman's love came to his aid. The powerful Russian Duchess Anna Ivanovna fell in love with him. She could swing the ducal election of Courland, and she offered to swing it Saxe's way if he would marry her.

Saxe told Adrienne of the offer. Heartbroken, the unselfish girl advised him to accept, which he did. As Duke of Courland and as husband of Anna Ivanovna, he would be one of the mighty potentates of Europe. It was an opportunity he could not resist. The way was clear.

And then Saxe spoiled everything—by another love-affair. One of Anna's maids of honor lost her heart to Saxe. He was glad of any variation from the ugly Russian duchess he was pledged to marry, and so he met the maid of honor's advances halfway.

Anna found it out. She also found out—what she could not and would not forgive—that Saxe had irreverently compared her unprepossessing face to a Westphalian ham. In fury she broke off her engagement, and she threw all the weight of her influence in Russia against Saxe. (Later she became the Czarina of Russia, ruling in her own right. Had Saxe refrained from playing the fool, he might thus have reigned with her as Czar of Russia and have founded an imperial dynasty.)

With Russia against him Saxe could not hold his dukedom. He fought like a lion with his handful of followers for nearly a year against the Russian hordes sent to oust him. But the odds were too great; crushed by weight of numbers, he gave up the useless struggle and returned to France—and to Adrienne.

"It took all Russia to beat me!" he announced modestly, as he returned to his post in the French army.

And Paris loudly applauded the boast.

BUT at heart Saxe was furious over his defeat. And he repaid Adrienne's love and generosity by venting his surly ill temper on her. He made her life a burden; he accused her—with utter falsehood—of infidelity to him. The poor girl bore his ill-treatment like an angel. Here is part of a letter she wrote to him at this time. It is worth reading:

> I am worn out with grief. I have wept all this livelong night. It is foolish of me, since I have nothing with which to reproach myself. But I can't endure to have you displeased with me. You suspect me, you accuse me! Oh, how can I convince you—you who alone have the power to wound my heart?

To add another drop to the sorrow-cup of Adrienne,—and incidentally to cause her death,—a new rival entered the lists and demanded Saxe's worthless love. The newcomer was Françoise Lorraine, Duchesse de Bouillon, a woman of royal blood and tiger-impulses. She fell in love with Saxe. Fidelity to Adrienne did not stand in Saxe's way—it never did; but the Duchess did not interest him. He told her so frankly.

Everyone knew of Saxe's affair with Adrienne. The Duchess decided that the actress alone stood in her way and that with Adrienne dead, Saxe would readily fall victim to her own charms. A few days later a man named Bouret came to see Adrienne and confessed that the Duchesse de Bouillon had paid him to send the actress a box of poisoned candies. He went on to say he had not the heart to commit such a crime. He offered the candies as proof of his story. The police fed one of the bonbons to a dog—and the beast died in agony.

The Duchess, accused of attempted poisoning, angrily denied her guilt. But three days later Adrienne was stricken with a mortal illness—evidently caused by poison.

As she lay dying, a priest was sent for. He was the Abbé Lanquet, curate of St. Sulpice. In those days, an actress was supposed to be by profession a hardened sinner. Before he would shrive Adrienne, the priest demanded that she renounce the stage "and all other sins." Dutifully she repeated the words after him. Next the priest intoned the question:

"Do you place your hope in the God of the universe?"

The dying girl did not answer. Her thoughts were straying. At the other side of the bed knelt Saxe, weeping his heart out. She laid a caressing hand on his bowed head and murmured unintelligible love-words to comfort him.

The priest frowned, and repeated his query:

"Do you place your hope in the God of the universe?"

A strange light overspread Adrienne's drawn face. Pointing ecstatically toward Saxe, she exclaimed:

"He is my hope—my universe—my god."

For which beautiful blasphemy she was allowed to die unshriven. Lanquet stamped away, declaring:

"There is no question of religious burial for that lost woman."

AFTER his first grief had spent itself, Saxe began to listen with less indifference to the allurements of the Duchesse de Bouillon. So the murder of Adrienne did not go for naught, after all. Saxe writes thus of the Duchess:

She had a mouth made for kisses. She was twenty-three years old, very beauteous, with delicate features, broad forehead, great black eyes with long lashes, a forest of brown hair. Married to a man forty years her senior, she had made the quest of love the chief purpose of her life. And there was not a path in the garden of life she had left unexplored.

Of Adrienne's death, by the way, the only comment in the autobiography is:

"As for me, well, I regretted her."

Which was the sole epitaph of the woman who had lost wealth and happiness and life for his sake.

During the next few years Saxe's fame spread throughout the world. He became the foremost general in Europe. He wrote a technical book on war which is still a military classic. He won for France the battle of Fontenoy—which, says Watson, postponed the French Revolution for nearly half a century. In this battle he was too ill to ride his horse, and he was carried about the field in a big wicker basket.

For his services Louis XV gave him a castle and a kingly pension and made him a Marshal of France.

Time was dragging on, and Saxe was growing old. He had long since jilted his early love, the Princesse de Conti. Now she sought revenge for her rejection. Aided by her son, she threw in Saxe's way every obstacle she could, and she all but ruined his power at court.

But now another woman came to his aid—Mme. de Pompadour, the all-potent favorite of King Louis. Between them she and Saxe routed the Contis and drove them from court. But Pompadour dared not show too strongly her fondness for the dashing Marshal. Her own position with the King was too precious—and too precarious—to risk it by an open affair, even with the hero of the hour.

Saxe's fickle heart next was caught by Mlle. Navarre, an actress. But now age and illness were stripping him of his Herculean strength and of his mysterious magnetic hold over women. For the first time a woman left him of her own accord. Mlle. Navarre got all the money she could from Saxe—then deserted him for the Chevalier de Mirabeau.

Saxe, in fury, followed the elopers. He was too feeble to fight duels as of yore. But Mirabeau dropped dead soon after Saxe overtook the pair. There were whispers that the once-invincible fighter had exchanged the sword for the poison-flask, but the charge was not pressed.

A woman named Verrières—whose father was a Paris lemonade-peddler—superseded Mlle. Navare. She soon learned to despise Saxe. Once she said:

"You are an old fool."

"I quite agree with you," he sighed. "Yet I will do one wise act."

The "wise act" was to dismiss her, with an annuity.

There is no profit in going on with the sordid list of loves that marked and marred Saxe's last years. There is less profit—and much sadness—in relating the story of any man whose splendid prowess has departed and who is drifting toward a miserable, diseased old age.

Saxe died rather suddenly on November, 30, 1750. His physicians said his death was caused by fever, but a story was current that his old sweetheart's son, the Prince of Conti, forced a duel upon him in the park of his castle and left him on the field mortally wounded. As he lay at the point of death, Saxe whispered to his doctor:

"My life has been beautiful. But it has been so short!"

"He died believing nothing and hoping even less," was Mme. de Pompadour's comment on hearing of his end.

Louis XV took the news less cynically. He cried aloud:

"Now there are no more generals left on earth—nothing but understrappers!"

She was Mme. Dudevant, better known as Georges Sand, the most famous woman author of her day.

VI — Frédéric Chopin
Invalid Heartbreaker

DOWN the main street of Nohant dashed a man in panic flight.

His long, gold-brown hair flew wild in the breeze. His beautiful, aquiline-nosed face—usually as pallid as death—was flushed with fear. Every weak muscle in his emaciated body was strained in the effort to escape from a big and swarthy woman who ran close behind him, brandishing a warming-pan and swearing at the top of her lungs.

The woman clenched a half-smoked cigar in her free hand. Her thick fingers were smeared with dried ink. She wore a mannish shirt, a pair of fiery red trousers and gay Turkish slippers. Her face was heavy and ugly. (Thomas Carlyle used to say it reminded him of a horse's.)

She was Mme. Dudevant,—better known, then and now, as Georges Sand,—the most famous woman author of her day in all Europe, and great-granddaughter, left-handedly, of Marshal Saxe. Her weird costume was merely a lounging-suit she wore when at work in her study. The cigar represented a habit that added to her masculinity. The man she pursued in this murderous fashion was her lover.

He was Frédéric Chopin. As he is the hero of this article, I am half-ashamed to introduce him to you in such an undignified moment of his love-life. It would have been more suitable to begin by depicting him at the piano, charming a hushed roomful of adoring women by playing dreamily one of his own glorious compositions.

But every hero has his off moments. And really, it was not Chopin's fault that a furious woman threatened to brain him with a warming-pan; the fault was hers. And thus menaced by a lady, Julius Caesar or Jess Willard or any other superman would have had no recourse but to take to his heels. So please don't blame poor Chopin for the frantically unpoetic way he has run into this story.

The bystanders, in the street, looked on with cynical amusement at the furious chase. It was no novelty to them. They had seen the same sort of thing more than once before, since the world-famous lovers had come out from Paris to Nohant for the summer.

People nowadays, seeing such a chase, would probably look around for the camera-man. But the Nohant folk knew better. They knew that the two temperamental (and too-temperamental) geniuses had clashed once more, and that as usual Chopin was having the worst of it.

Balzac heard of the warming-pan race and of other scenes of the same type. And he wrote to a friend:

> I fear Chopin is an incorrigible flirt. But as for Georges Sand, she certainly does not behave always like a perfect gentleman!

NOW, if I have managed to hook your interest, will you let me drop Georges Sand for a few moments—she comes in again later—and begin with Chopin's earlier and less violent love-affairs?

Frédéric Chopin—soul of fire in a fragile consumptive body—was of the true woman-tamer breed. He numbered his conquests not by dozens but by the hundred—this delicate Polish genius! Almost no woman could resist him. It is not on record that many of them tried to.

As a composer and as a pianist, and in his own life, he breathed the strangely poetic and infinitely tragic spirit of Poland. As to his conquests, they are best summed up by his French biographer, who says:

> He found himself unable to avoid stepping on some of the numberless hearts that were flung like roses at his feet. He could modulate from one love-affair to another as fleetly and gracefully as from one piano-key to its most remote neighbor.

It was not by any conscious effort of his own that he made women love him. It was not through his own wish that he was forever falling in love. He was fated to love and to be loved—because he had been born so.

When he was a boy, still in his late teens, he met Leopoldine Blahetka—his first real sweetheart whose name is recorded. She was a musician, older than Chopin and already recognized in the world of music. She fell in love, before she half-realized it, with the dreamy boy-genius.

As far as Leopoldine was concerned, it was a really serious affair. In it she concentrated all her heart and her temperament. Mingled with her love for the lad was an amazed reverence for his almost uncanny prowess as a musician.

But Chopin, as soon as he found how easily she was to be won, tired of her. The end was hastened by the appearance of a rival on the scene—a rival of Leopoldine's, not of Chopin's.

The newcomer was Princess Elisa Radziwell, whose father at that time was the young man's patron. The Princess took piano-lessons from Chopin and lost her heart to him. Chopin returned the compliment, and for a while the romance budded promisingly.

But it came to nothing. In those days even the most inspired musician could not aspire to the hand of a princess, and Elisa's father made this dour fact so plain to Chopin that the affair (and the acquaintanceship as well) broke off then and there.

Chopin had his revenge—a petty one, but the only form of revenge then in stock for such a case as his.

Elisa's father invited him to a state dinner. As soon as the meal was over, he bade Chopin play the piano for his guests.

"But I have eaten so little!" protested Chopin whimsically—bowing and leaving the house.

Elisa did not recover, as did he, from the ruin of her dream. She pined away and soon afterward died.

Both these episodes—and a desperate but sordid affair with a waitress—were over and done with before Chopin was twenty.

With an experience already ranging from a princess to a servant, he was a graduate student in the school of love. And it was just before his twentieth birthday—in 1829—that he met, at Warsaw, Constantia Gladovska, a noted concert-singer. At sight he fell madly in love with her. He heard her sing, and after the concert he sent a friend to her with this ardent message:

"Tell her that as long as my heart continues to beat, I shall not cease to adore her. Tell her that even after my death my ashes shall be strewn under her little feet."

For the first time, perhaps for the only time, he was exerting himself to make a woman love him. He gave Constantia no rest, but was forever calling upon her or waylaying her in the street or sending her an avalanche of notes or writing music to her. She was the inspiration of some of his greatest early music. To his love for her we owe his

Chopin heard Constantia sing and sent a friend to her with this ardent message:
"Tell her that as long as my heart continues to beat, I shall not cease to adore her. Tell her that even after my death my ashes shall be strewn under her little feet."

immortal "Concerto in E Minor" and several other deathless works.

For more than a year he wooed Constantia. For her sake he gave up his dream of leaving Poland and of spreading his fame as a pianist through Europe. Constantia, for a while, was carried off her feet by this whirlwind courtship. But she was a placid, commonsensible soul; and when a rich merchant named Grabowski asked her to marry, she cheerfully threw Chopin over and took the wealthier man.

CHOPIN was heartbroken. He shook the dust of Warsaw from his feet, turned his back on the fickle and thrifty Constantia and went to Paris to live. It was the best thing that ever happened to him. Much sob-stuff has been written, denouncing Constantia's treatment of her genius-lover. But at twenty-one heart-wounds are quick to heal. And like many another jilted lover, Chopin was driven forth to wealth and reputation by his loss. He speedily consoled himself.

For in Paris he met Delphine, the beautiful young Countess Potocka, whom he had known slightly in her girlhood at Warsaw. Then began a strange affair that lasted, off and on, to the very hour of Chopin's death—an affair as exquisite and unearthly as a winter sunset. Delphine loved her elderly husband and—presumably—was true to him. But she lavished upon Chopin an adoration that was more like that of a mother to a sick child than that of a sweetheart.

She had a divine voice, a voice that had a strangely soothing effect on Chopin. He used to send for her, to sing softly to him, when he was ill or nervous or out of temper. And always the singing brought him an exalted calm and peace.

Delphine was always at his side—even at the end—when most he needed her. And she effaced herself when other women claimed his wayward fancy—as they usually did. When Chopin died, she helped to support his parents as long as they lived. In serene old age she wrote her autobiography. The second sentence of the book announces, with a certain reminiscent pride: "I was the intimate friend of the illustrious Chopin!"

A LITTLE after he came to Paris, Chopin went on a visit to Dresden, where he met Marie Wodzinska. Again he lost his heart. By way of variety, he actually asked Marie to be his wife.

She was willing enough, but her family had other ideas for her. They wanted her to make a brilliant marriage; they saw in Chopin nothing but a poor and eccentric piano-player. They forbade the match.

And again Chopin was in luck, for he and Marie had planned that after marriage he was to settle down at Warsaw as a plodding music-teacher. So for the second time fate with a heartbreak whip scourged him forth from domestic happiness to greatness.

Back to Paris went the forlorn Chopin. And Marie was wed to a Polish count named Skarbek. The union was not happy and soon ended in a divorce. The husband, when he was asked why he and his wife had not gotten on better together, replied curtly:

"She plays too much Chopin music!" Which may have meant anything or nothing—or everything.

Paris greeted the returning Chopin with as much enthusiasm as if he had been a national hero. His music was the most popular of the day. His presence was sought at every kind of social function. His piano recitals were jammed to the doors—though he never received more than three hundred dollars for any one recital. Women went mad over him.

Whereat he began to wax still more eccentric. One of his new eccentricities took the form of cranky foppishness in dress. For example, according to E. S. Smith:

> None of his clothes pleased him. No tailor could win from him a word of approval. Before every concert several evening coats were ordered at different tailors. All were bad; none would fit.
> At the last moment before appearing on the stage Chopin would seize the coat of his friend and pupil Gutmann (twice his size) and appear in it.
> His love of exquisite manners and breeding was, it may be, pushed too far; but he was disgusted and irritated by those artists who laid claim to genius on the strength of neglected dress and disordered hair. Whatever money he had was always dispersed in doing good or in giving pleasure.

ONE evening in 1837 Chopin went to a reception. Halfway up the stairs he halted and said to a man at his side: "A violet-scented phantom is following me. It means misfortune. I am going to turn back."

He was laughed out of this odd fancy, and continued his way to the drawing-room. The first person he saw in the crowd gathered there, was a woman—mannish of air, dark and rugged of feature. Turning again to the man at his side, he said:

"I do not like her face. Something in it repels me. Who is she?"

"She is Mme. Dudevant—Georges Sand, the novelist," answered his friend.

"I do not want to meet her!" exclaimed Chopin with an uncontrollable shudder.

But he did meet her—almost at once. And the ill-matched pair proceeded without delay to fall in love with each other. It was the love of Chopin's life, and the most lasting of Georges Sand's countless loves.

It would have been hard to find two people worse matched. Chopin was fragile, an invalid, ethereal. Georges Sand was his opposite in every way. She was not even pretty. She was crazily vain and brutally selfish.

Long before he met Georges Sand Chopin had been stricken with consumption. He was mortally ill. His friends expected him to die at any time. But this strange new love-affair had a miraculous effect on him. He grew stronger and in better health than his doctors had deemed possible. The hand of death had been upon him. A woman's buoyantly aggressive vitality smote the dread hand aside.

"It is your magnificent strength, madame," said a flattering doctor, "which is keeping life in him."

Georges Sand's egregious vanity was touched by the queer speech. She went around repeating it to her friends as a tribute to her marvelous powers. She even proclaimed herself a martyr, for squandering her precious vital force in preserving Chopin's life. Poetical Paris applauded. Cynical Paris chuckled.

So began a romance that lasted for ten long years, and that was kept up with no show of secrecy.

In the first flush of self-sacrifice, Georges Sand took Chopin to the island of Majorca, hoping to cure his lungs. There the bad weather and worse food and lack of music all played havoc with the sick man's nerves. Georges Sand's temper had always been bad. Now that the early glamour of her love was wearing off she found life with a consumptive not all a bed of roses. And the series of spectacular quarrels began that ended only with the end of the love-affair itself.

There were always dramatic and tearful reconciliations, however, followed soon by new quarrels. In one of these reconciliations Chopin said he was a dying man and begged her to make him supremely happy by marrying him. She refused; and another lurid quarrel set in.

Back to France came the pair after a wretched winter at Majorca. Georges Sand complained loudly to her sympathetic friends that she was sacrificing everything to "that detestable invalid." She announced to all and sundry that Chopin was fretful and selfish and impossible to get along with, and that she herself was an angel of patient devotion. Chopin said nothing at all—in public.

Yet the return to Paris did not sever the odd bond. The relationship went on for years. Georges Sand was forever making "copy" of her sweethearts' lives. Of Chopin's winter with her at Majorca and of his past amours she wrote:

> The poor great artist was a wretched patient..... Once he took a fancy to the granddaughter of a celebrated Parisian maestro. He thought of asking her in marriage, at the same time that he entertained the idea of another marriage in Poland—his loyalty engaged nowhere and his fickle heart floating from one person to another.
> The young Parisian received him very kindly, and all went as well as could be till, on going to visit her one day (in company with another musician who was of more note in Paris than he at that time), she offered a chair to this other gentleman before thinking of inviting Chopin to be seated.
> He never called on her again, and he forgot her immediately!

MME. SAND also gives an account of Chopin's mode of work. I shall quote it in full, if you will let me—first because it is worth reading, to show how a genius toiled and with what tedious effort Chopin's golden melodies were born, and second because it may encourage workers along all lines to know of the difficulties a fellow-craftsman overcame. The account runs:

> His creation of music was spontaneous and miraculous. He found it without seeking it, without foreseeing it. It came in his piano suddenly complete, sublime—or it sang in his head during a walk, and he was impatient to play it to himself.
> But then began the most heartrending labor I ever saw. It was a series of efforts of irresolution and of frettings to seize again certain details of the theme he had heard. What he had conceived as a whole he analyzed too much, when wishing to write it; and his regret in not finding it again threw him into a fit of despair.
> He shut himself up in his room for whole days—weeping, walking, breaking his pens, repeating and altering a bar a hundred times, writing and effacing it as many times and recommencing the next day with a minute and desperate perseverance.
> He spent six weeks over a single page—only to write it at last as he had noted it down at the very first..... Chopin showed temper when I disturbed him. And when angry, he was alarming.

The Woman Tamers

Chopin's Georges Sand affair was not all storm and stress. There were times of calm when it shone forth in rose-colored light. And there were bits of humor flecked throughout its ten-year course too. For instance:

Georges Sand had a puppy that Chopin had given her. The pup spent most of its time running around in circles, chasing its own tail. One evening as this ridiculous chase was going on in the drawing-room the woman suggested to her lover:

"Why don't you set the doggie to music?"

On the instant Chopin crossed to the piano, sat down and composed his wonderful "Waltz in D Flat" (Opus 64)—the melody of which, as a critic has said, "moves in swift, erratic circles, chasing itself up and down the keyboard."

The affair at last wore itself out through its own increasing bitterness. After one mad quarrel, Georges Sand deserted Chopin. It was a crushing blow to him. A thousand times she had promised she would stay beside him to the inevitable end, and that he should die in her arms.

She wrote this bitter excuse for their parting, wherein she summed up in a single sentence the keynote of their ten-year life together:

> We never but once addressed a single reproach to each other—and that was from the first to the last time we met!

But they were to meet once more, he and she, just once. It was at a musicale in a Paris salon. Georges Sand saw Chopin standing alone in one corner of the room. A biographer thus describes what followed:

> Thinking no one observed her, she went up to him and held out her hand, murmuring in a voice she thought was audible to him alone:
> "Frédéric!"
> He saw her familiar form standing there before him. She was penitent, subdued, seeking reconciliation. Chopin's handsome face turned deathly pale. Without a word, he left the room.

Le Gallienne is one of the woman's few defenders. He writes:

> Actually it seems to me that Georges Sand gave more to Chopin than she ever received in return. With her own burden of genius to carry, she attempted lovingly and faithfully to carry his too, through ten of the most fruitful years

of his life. And we (who care nowadays more for his music than for her books) should gratefully remember this, to her everlasting credit.

AFTER that chance meeting with Georges Sand, Chopin lost his grip on life. He avoided society, but could not avoid the women who would not let him alone. These followed him everywhere, even besieging his rooms.

He was in no mood to seek the consolation they offered. He was dying, and he was dying in something very like poverty, for he had squandered his money as fast as he had earned it. An English girl—Miss Sterling—who loved him, heard of his plight. And she sent him, anonymously, enough money to keep him in comfort for the few weeks that remained.

Delphine Potocka, too, heard he was dying. From Warsaw to the Riviera she hastened, to make ready a house for him in which he could convalesce. Then she rushed to Paris to nurse him back to health.

She arrived one bitter October day in 1847, just before he died. Opening his eyes, Chopin smiled feebly up at her and whispered:

"Sing to me!"

For the last time the wonderful voice that had always soothed and charmed away his sorrows brought its magic to Chopin's aid. Softly, with infinite sweetness, Delphine sang for him Stradella's "Canticle of the Virgin."

"It is heaven!" murmured Chopin when the golden voice had ceased. "Once more!"

Just then his pupil Gutmann came into the room. He had been sent to tell Georges Sand that her former lover was dying and that he was calling incessantly for her. And Gutmann had been forced to come back without the heartless woman he had gone to fetch. Chopin read in the man's face the failure of his mission. The dying man cried aloud in sharp anguish:

"She promised I should die in no arms but hers!"

Over and over he sobbed out the bitter plaint. That night he died.

Seven different women later vowed publicly that Chopin had died in their arms. Delphine Potocka made no such claim. She had no need to.

Appendix

Source Material Notes

These essays and illustrations originally ran in six consecutive issues of Green Book magazine, from February through July of 1918.

February 1918

Front text (accompanying the portrait of Albert Payson Terhune that appears at the front of this book):

THE author of "Dollars and Cents," "The Years of the Locust" and "The White Way" has written for THE GREEN BOOK MAGAZINE a series of stories entitled "The Woman Tamers"—stories of men who have possessed that queer power of winning the heart of every woman they chose to attract. The first of these stories, that of Lord Byron, begins on the opposite page. Next month Mr. Terhune will write about the amorous adventures of Napoleon.

Front text (preceding the essay):

ONE man has the queer power of winning the heart of every woman he chooses to captivate—and of many a woman whom he doesn't. Why? Another man, of better looks, manner and attainments, finds it impossible to rouse from womankind a warmer sentiment than a tepid friendly interest. Why?

John Wilkes, ugliest man in Europe, claimed—and proved his claim—that he could enthrall any woman after a fifteen-minute chat. Byron—lame, fickle, coarse—was the darling of a hundred women. Dean Swift—the *Gulliver* man—was repulsive, and was a physical defective. Yet he was the hero of some of the most romantic love-episodes in history. And so on down—or up—the line.

The only answer seems to be: "One man in a thousand is a born woman-tamer. And he is a born woman-tamer, for no reason that his less lucky fellow-men can find out."

In this series I am going to recount the love-lives—or so much of them as is tellable—of some of the world's foremost woman-tamers. I shall not deal with the historical side of their stories, but merely with their heart-adventures. It will not be profitable reading, but even a literary novice could not fail to make it interesting.

End text:
Next month: "Napoleon as a Woman-Tamer."

March 1918
End text:
The strange amatory career of Jonathan Swift, who wrote "Gulliver's Travels" and many other famous satires, will be the subject of the next article in Mr. Terhune's series "The Woman-Tamers." It will appear in our next issue.

April 1918
End text:
(The love-affairs of Alexandre Dumas, author of "The Three Musketeers" and many other noted novels, will be described by Albert Payson Terhune in our next issue.)

Terhune makes the following reference:
"Kennedy once wrote of 'the Terrible Meek.'"
This refers to a one-act play, "The Terrible Meek," by Charles Rann Kennedy (1808–1867), published in 1912.

May 1918
End text:
The love-adventures of Marshal Saxe, a noted warrior and heart-breaker, will be described in the next of Mr. Terhune's fascinating articles.

June 1918

End text:
The love-adventures of Marshal Saxe, a noted warrior and heart-breaker, will be described in the next of Mr. Terhune's fascinating articles.

July 1918

End text:
Next month Mr. Terhune writes of the interesting love-affairs of Frederic Chopin.

Revision made for this edition:
BUT as heart Saxe was furious
(was changed to)
BUT at heart Saxe was furious

General notes

Captions accompanying illustrations are as published.

Jess Willard is mentioned twice in these articles. Willard (1881 to 1968) was a boxing champion with the nickname "Pottawatomie Giant." He was strong and could take lots of punishment. He lost his heavyweight boxing championship title to Jack Dempsey in 1919.

Some word usage and punctuation might strike today's educated reader as being unusual. However, the text has been left mostly unchanged, to retain the flavor of the original work.

One idiosyncrasy that *was* changed for this edition is the spelling of "wont" to "won't" when indicating "will not." The Publisher considered this *too* outrageously outré to let stand.

Other books available
from the Silver Creek Press

2016
In Treason's Track, by Albert Payson Terhune
A novel of the American Revolution.

2015
The Flood Fighters, by Albert Payson Terhune
A novel first serialized in Country Gentleman magazine in 1920, published under a pseudonym and not reprinted until now.

An Albert Payson Terhune Reader
27 stories by Terhune from pulp magazines of the 1910s and 20s, featuring all original illustrations.

(The above are available from the major bookstores online, both as hardcopy books and as e-books.)

2006
The Park Avenue Hunt Club:
The Silver Creek Edition
by Judson Phillips and Rodney Schroeter
(Available from the publisher)

Forthcoming
More work by Albert Payson Terhune
that has not seen print since its original publication.

More pulp fiction from the early 20th Century
by various authors.

www.ingramcontent.com/pod-product-compliance
Lightning Source LLC
Chambersburg PA
CBHW070550300426
44113CB00011B/1855